AMERICAN

AMERICAN
ISLAM

GROWING UP
MUSLIM IN AMERICA

Richard Wormser

WALKER & COMPANY
NEW YORK

First published in the United States of America in 1994 by Walker Publishing Company, Inc.; first paperback edition published in 2002.

Published simultaneously in Canada by Fitzhenry and Whiteside, Markham, Ontario L3R 4T8

Library of Congress Cataloging-in-Publication Data
Wormser, Richard, 1933–
American Islam : growing up Muslim in America / Richard Wormser.
p.   cm.
Includes bibliographical references.
ISBN 0-8027-8343-0. — ISBN 0-8027-8344-9 (reinforced)
1. Islam—United States.   I. Title.
BP67.U6W67   1994
297'.0973—dc20   94-12335
CIP

ISBN 0-8027-7628-0 (paperback)

All quotations are from interviews with students throughout the United States. At the request of some of them, we have used only their first names.

There is no uniform way of spelling Arabic words in English. The name of the founder of Islam may be spelled Muhammad (the most common form), Mohammed, Muhammed, etc. We have tried to use spellings agreed upon by most scholars.

For information about permission to reproduce selections from this book, write to Permissions, Walker & Company, 435 Hudson Street, New York, New York 10014

BOOK DESIGN BY CLAIRE NAYLON VACCARO

Visit Walker & Company's Web site at www.walkerbooks.com

Printed in the United States of America

2   4   6   8   10   9   7   5   3   1

Contents

$\mathcal{P}$ART I

BECOMING AMERICAN,
REMAINING MUSLIM

Contents

PART II
ISLAM IN THE AFRICAN-AMERICAN COMMUNITY

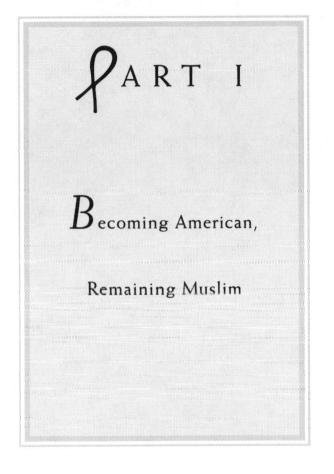

Part I

Becoming American,

Remaining Muslim

1.

Islam and the West: The Roots

of an Ancient Conflict

"*I*'m proud to be an American and I hate Arabs and I always have."

The speaker was a nineteen-year-old anti-Arab demonstrator in Chicago several days after Islamic militants deliberately and maliciously crashed two planes into the World Trade Center in New York killing some three thousand people. Their acts, combined with the crashing of a third plane into the Pentagon building in Washington, D.C., triggered a wave of violence against Muslim Americans in cities, towns, and high schools and on college campuses throughout the United States.

In Dallas, Texas, a Molotov cocktail bomb was hurled against an Islamic center. In Chicago, a Muslim building was bombed. In California, a Muslim gas station attendant was attacked with a machete. In New York, a man tried to run over a Muslim woman parking attendant because he claimed that she was "trying to destroy my country." In Illinois, two Muslim women students were beaten up. In Louisiana, a Congressman said that it was perfectly acceptable that the FBI intensively investigate people who wear "a diaper on their heads," referring to the scarf many Muslims wear as headcover. (He later apologized.) In Arizona, a gunman shot and killed the Sikh owner of a gas station believing he was Muslim (he was not). The killer tried to justify his act by shouting, "I'm a patriot, I'm damn American all the way."

The irony is that the overwhelming majority of Muslims living in America condemned the attacks on the World Trade Center and the Pentagon. They also condemned all acts of terrorism and have publicly supported peace efforts in the Middle East.

Even though most Americans and their political and religious leaders condemn attacks on America's Muslims, Muslims have been subjected to prejudice even before the most recent incidents. In times of crisis, they have been cursed, picketed, threatened, occasionally beaten, and even murdered because they practice the same religion as a relative small number of people who have committed acts of violence. They have been portrayed unflatteringly in movies, television programs, books, and cartoons as "oil sheiks" traveling to gambling casinos, religious fanatics, magicians with evil powers, and terrorists killing innocent people. When Muslims are accused of crimes, unlike other religious groups, they are often identified by their religion—"Muslims Battle Police," for example.

One consequence of this bad publicity is that many Americans believe that Islam is a primitive, violent religion, intolerant of non-Muslims, and demeaning to women. A recent study published by the American Muslim Council revealed that of all the religious groups surveyed, Muslims have the lowest favorable rating and highest unfavorable rating. Only 23 percent of people interviewed had a good impression of Islam, while 36 percent had negative feelings. The remaining 41 percent were not sure. By comparison, the average ratings for Catholics and Protestants were 64 percent favorable and 15 percent unfavorable. The most serious charges made against Muslims is that they are "fanatics" and that this fanaticism breeds terrorism.

The hostility of the West toward Islam is nothing new. For almost 700 years, until the twentieth century, Muslims and Christians were in a constant state of war. Muslims have been hated and feared ever since Muslim armies first invaded many of the areas ruled by Christians almost 1,400 years ago. Christian Europe, ignorant of the origins of Islam and the beliefs of Muslims, feared and hated the new religion. The Roman Catholic church considered Islam a perversion of Christianity and regarded Islam's founder, the prophet Muhammad (whom Catholics called Mahout), as the anti-Christ, the devil incarnate. The fact that Muslims conquered and ruled Jerusalem, the most Holy Christian city, was intolerable to them. In the year 1095, Pope Innocent II called for a crusade against Islam. He said it would be a righteous war, favored by God. Those who fell in battle would be granted absolution of their sins and a place in heaven. The crowds who heard his message were ecstatic. They shouted, *"Die lo volt"* (God wills it) and hurried home to pack their knapsacks and weapons. From all over Europe, hundreds of thousands of men, women, and children, from nobles and knights to beggars and prostitutes, joined the crusade to free Jerusalem from the Muslim "infidels."

The Muslims had ruled the Middle East with tolerance. While they saw themselves as the bearers of God's truth and the only truly legitimate power on earth, Muslims protected Christians and Jews under their jurisdiction. They considered them "People of the Book," the forerunners of Islam, and granted them a place in the community. Although Christians and Jews were taxed more than Muslims and suffered some legal restrictions in dress and occupation, they were allowed to practice their religion and conduct business without serious interference. The opposite

This medieval painting shows the conquest of Jerusalem by the Christians in 1099. Fifty years later the Muslims recaptured the holy city. It remained in Muslim hands until the First World War.

was never the case. No Muslim would have been allowed to live in medieval Europe. Muslims would have been burned at the stake as heretics, driven into exile, or forced to convert to Christianity.

Muslim tolerance did not impress the Crusaders. Setting out for the Holy Land, they first marched across Europe and the eastern Roman Empire (now Greece and Turkey), slaughtering and pillaging as they went. Their favorite target was the Jews, whom they massacred by the thousands. They also slaughtered anyone else who objected to or resisted their robbing fellow Christians. In 1097, to Europe's relief, the Crusaders finally arrived in the

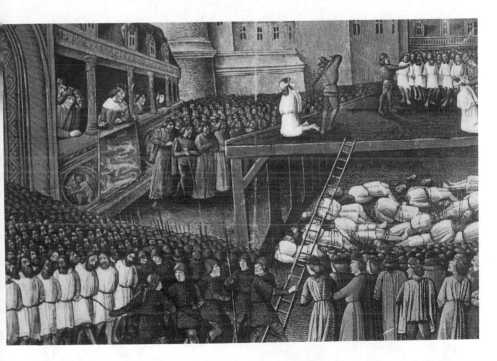

This medieval Christian painting shows Crusaders massacring Muslim civilians, including women and children. Muslims, by comparison, while fierce in battle, tended to spare the lives of innocents.

Middle East. They defeated the Muslim armies in a series of battles until they arrived at the gates of Jerusalem. One Muslim warrior, Usamah Ibn-Munqidit, recorded his observations about his Christian enemy:

> *Their soldiers are of mighty courage and in the hour of combat do not think of flight but prefer death. But you shall see none more filthy than they. They do not cleanse or bathe themselves more than once or twice a year, and then in cold water, and they do not wash their garments from the time they put them on till they fall to pieces. They are a people of treachery and mean character.*

In 1099, Jerusalem fell. The Crusaders spared no one. Violating the rules of warfare, they slaughtered civilians—women and

This Islamic painting from Persia represents a Muslim school. Muslims placed a great deal of emphasis on learning and produced many great scientists and poets.

children, Muslims and Jews. Raymond of Aguiles, one of the conquering lords who chronicled the Crusades, glorified the massacre:

> *Wonderful sights to be seen. Some of our men, and those were the more merciful, cut off the heads of their enemies; others tortured them longer by casting them into the flames . . . men rode on blood up to their knees and bridle reins. Indeed it was a just and splendid judgment of God that this place shall be filled with the blood of the unbelievers.*

While Muslims could also be terrible in battle, they were usually more humane than their enemies. When the legendary Muslim general Salah ad-Din reconquered Jerusalem in the twelfth century, he permitted the Christians to leave the city with most of their possessions.

By the time the Crusades were launched, Muslims had already built a great civilization centered on Islam, a civilization far superior in culture and science to that of the West. Despite the rise and fall of various Muslim empires, science, art, and literature flourished at different times throughout the Muslim world, reaching extraordinary heights in India, Persia, Iraq, Spain, and Egypt. One distinct feature of Islamic civilization was its universal Arabic language. The *Quran* (the Muslim holy book) had been revealed to Muhammad in Arabic, and Muslims originally refused to allow it to be translated into another language to avoid introducing errors into the text. (This position was later modified.) Converts to Islam had to learn to read and recite the Quran in Arabic. Almost all peoples living under Muslim rule, even Jews and Christians, found it was to their advantage to speak Arabic. Arabic letters and quotations from the Quran were highly stylized by calligraphic artists and used to decorate buildings, art objects, and furniture.

Islamic civilization was so influential that even while Christians were fighting Muslims, they were also learning from them. Muslims had discovered the most advanced knowledge in mathematics, astronomy, and medicine. They had developed the system of Arabic numerals, and a mathematician by the name of Muhammad ibn Musa al-Khawarazmi had invented a form of mathematics known in Arabic as *al-jaber*, which every student learns today as algebra. Christian monks journeyed to the great Muslim universities in Spain to copy the latest medical, scientific, and philosophic manuscripts, which they later translated into Latin. At a time when few Europeans could read or write, there

This French painting shows the French army invading Algeria in the nineteenth century. France would occupy the country for over one hundred years until the Algerians successfully rebelled.

were 400,000 manuscripts in the library of Cordoba, Spain, alone.

By the fifteenth century, it was Europe's turn to be threatened by Muslim armies. A new Muslim force, the Ottoman Turks, built an empire that extended into eastern Europe. In 1453, the Turks captured Constantinople, the former capital of the Byzantine Empire, which had resisted conquest for almost 800 years. They eventually renamed it Istanbul. In the sixteenth century, Turkish armies entered eastern Europe. By the seventeenth century, they were outside the gates of Vienna, Austria. Throughout Europe, churches were packed with people praying for deliverance from the "terrible Turks." Their prayers were answered. Vienna held fast, and the Turkish tide slowly receded. By 1700, the Turks were no longer a threat to the West.

Even as Ottoman armies dominated the world, Europeans were experiencing major revolutions in science, art, industry, and commerce. European ships sailed around the world in search of wealth and additional markets. European armies developed new and powerful weapons. By the eighteenth century, when the Ottomans realized what was happening, it was too late to catch up.

In 1793, a century after the Turks had been stopped for the last time at Vienna, the French emperor Napoleon Bonaparte invaded Egypt and easily defeated the Egyptian army. The Muslim world was now forced to yield to Western military and economic power. The West no longer regarded Muslims as infidels. Religion had yielded to the social sciences. Now Muslims were "backward" and "primitive." Their religion was considered "fanatical." The West saw its mission as "civilizing the barbarian." Its major method was gunpowder.

In 1830, French gunboats shelled the city of Algiers in Algeria as French tourists watched the bombardment from a nearby ship and applauded. The French celebrated their conquest as a victory of Christianity over Islam—the final crusade. General Saint Arnaud justified the conquest and the slaughter on the grounds of civilizing the Muslims.

> *We kill, we slaughter. The screaming of the terror-stricken blends with the noise of beasts that moan and groan from all sides. Little does it matter that France in her pitiful conduct goes beyond the limits of common morality. The essential thing is that she shall establish a lasting colony, and that, as a consequence, will bring European civilization to barbaric countries.*

Britain was quick to follow France. By 1890, its army had occupied Egypt and its navy established a military protectorate over the coastal gulf states. France occupied Tunisia and Morocco. During World War I, England and France divided the rest of the Middle East between them, with Britain claiming everything but Syria. Oil had recently been discovered in Iraq and the Arabian peninsula, and the Western powers made sure that they would be the ones to control it.

Until the Western invasion of the Middle East, no Muslim would have thought of migrating to the West. As Western influence spread throughout the Middle East, Muslims began to visit Europe for the first time in Islam's history. Most went to learn Western ways of doing things in order to bring this knowledge back to their own country. But as economic opportunities diminished in the Middle East, a small number of Muslims left to make better lives for themselves and their families in the West.

Emigration from the Middle East to America began in 1869 when a group of Muslims from Yemen arrived soon after the completion of the Suez Canal in Egypt. In 1875, both Christian and Muslim immigrants came to the United States from Syria, Lebanon, Jordan, and Palestine. Muslims were also emigrating from Poland, Russia, Albania, and Yugoslavia. By 1914, Muslims from sixty countries had settled in America.

Like millions of other immigrants to this country, most Muslims came here to find "gold in the streets"—that is, to make a living, prosper, and one day return to their homelands. They worked as peddlers, miners, and factory laborers or opened up small stores and shops. They lived in communities with their fellow immigrants. They also experienced a great deal of anxiety. Strangers in a strange land, they lacked *mosques* (buildings for public worship) and *imams* (leaders to guide them in prayer). They hoped that enough of their people would emigrate to form a strong Muslim community in America. But after the First World War, the United States began to restrict immigration on racial grounds. Muslims were discriminated against and often denied entry.

Muslims began to establish religious communities despite the suspicion and occasional hostility of Americans unfamiliar with their religion. Some settled in the Midwest, where the first known mosque in America was built by immigrants in Ross, North Dakota, in 1929. The oldest standing mosque, in Cedar Rapids, Iowa, was converted into a mosque from a community center in 1934.

Not all of the Muslims who came here kept their faith, however. The biggest threat to the Muslim community in America came from within. Many Muslim immigrants found they enjoyed the American way of life. They preferred to remain in the United States rather than return to their own countries. Many abandoned Islam. One immigrant described what happened: "They began drinking beer and eating pork in order to become good Americans. Many slipped into the mainstream of American culture and gave up their Islamic way of life. They changed their names. Muhammad became Michael and Salam, Samuel. They kept their religion a secret."

Until the 1960s, most Americans were unaware of the existence of what was then a relatively small Muslim presence in America. But as wars, civil wars, and revolutions erupted throughout the Islamic world, Muslims began to immigrate to the United States by the hundreds of thousands. There were Palestinian refugees escaping from the conflict with Israel; refugees from Lebanon and Afghanistan fleeing the terrors of civil wars; Iranians escaping the militancy of religious rule in their country; Indian and Kashmiri Muslims fearful of the growing hostility against them in India; and Muslims from Pakistan, Bangladesh, and eastern Europe seeking economic opportunity in the United States.

Most of these new arrivals maintained a strong ethnic and religious identity. They lived among their own ethnic groups and tried to re-create their culture in America. Their neighborhoods were filled with a variety of stores and restaurants that sold the products from their countries (clothing, music, books, and food). They practiced Islam faithfully. But as their children became Americanized, parents sometimes found themselves in conflict with them. Their major concern was whether their children would be able to maintain their religion in America. Though some were dismayed to find their children rejected Islam in favor of the values of modern pop culture, most were relieved to learn that their children's faith was strengthened by living in America. As one teenager stated, "There is no better place to practice Islam than in the United States."

2.

Islam—Its Origins and Practice

o one," says Ahmad Hassan, an Egyptian student, "can understand what Islam means to us without having some understanding of what we believe and the importance of the prophet Muhammad in our lives. Yet, despite the differences, there are many points of contact between us and Judaism and Christianity. There's a lot of things we share which could unite us rather than separate us."

Islam—like Judaism and Christianity—was born in the harsh, desert lands of the Middle East. In Egypt, Moses led the Jewish people out of bondage. In Nazareth, Jesus Christ was born, and in Jerusalem, he was crucified. Near Mecca, in the Arabian peninsula, the prophet Muhammad gave the Arabian people Islam. These three holy men—who had much in common—founded the faiths and ideals that almost two billion people believe today.

Muhammad was born to a poor family around the year A.D. 570 in the town of Mecca. Mecca was then famous as a trading center and for its many religious shrines that the Arabian tribes held sacred. When Muhammad was a child, his parents died and

There are approximately 1,000 mosques in the United States today, although the majority are not as elegant as this mosque in New York City.

he was adopted by an uncle, Abu Talib. As a young man, Muhammad worked for a rich widow named Khadija, whom he eventually married.

One day, in about A.D. 610, Muhammad had a dream while in a mountain cave. In the dream, the angel Gabriel (called Jibril in Arabic) appeared and revealed to Muhammad words that were to become the first words of the Quran, the holy book of Muslims which they believe contains the revealed word of God. Shortly after the dream, Muhammad heard a voice say to him, "You are a messenger of God!" "I was standing," Muhammad was reported to have said, "but I fell on my knees and dragged myself along while the upper part of my chest was trembling." Khadija believed in him and encouraged him to preach his newfound faith to a few friends and neighbors.

Gradually, Muhammad publicized his teachings and tried to persuade his tribe, the Quraysh, to accept them. The new faith was called Islam, which means "submission." His followers were known as Muslims, "those who submit." The heart of this new religion was submission to Allah, the one true God. According to Muhammad, human beings have one basic choice in life. They can either accept Allah and worship him or reject him and suffer the consequences. Those who obey will be allowed into paradise on Judgment Day. Those who deny Allah will be doomed to eternal punishment in Hell. Even those who accept Islam are not automatically granted entrance to heaven. They will be judged by their good and bad deeds and rewarded or punished accordingly.

Muhammad said that throughout human history Allah had sent prophets to warn the people of God's punishment and reveal his love. A number of these messengers were sent to the Jews, including Moses, Daniel, David, and Jesus Christ, who Muhammad said was not divine but a prophet. Because Jews and Christians had not listened to or properly understood their prophets, Allah sent Muhammad—the last of his prophets—to the Arabian peoples with the true and final message. While he was a holy man, he was also a warrior, a diplomat, a husband, and a father who enjoyed the pleasures that life had to offer.

Muhammad demanded that the Arabs give up their old gods and submit to Allah. Although Muhammad first spoke to the Arabian people, Islam was a universal religion intended for everyone. Muhammad's message angered the rich and powerful people of Mecca. They were furious that he opposed the old gods. His opponents talked of killing him. In 622, Muhammad, for his own safety, migrated to the oasis of Yathrib (present-day

Medina), where he came into contact with a number of Jewish tribes. He tried to convince them that he was a prophet and that they should accept him as God's messenger and convert to Islam. He said that Islam was not a new religion but a fulfillment of the Jewish-Christian tradition. But the Jewish tribes refused to give up Judaism for Islam. Muhammad then dropped some of the Jewish customs he had adopted and announced that Islam was the last prophetic revelation. It was the supreme and definitive religion. Later, Muhammad drove many of the Jewish tribes out of Medina because he felt they opposed him.

Muhammad was aware that Jews and Christians had their own holy books in which God revealed himself to them. Muhammad said that Allah had revealed himself through the Quran. Since the Quran was of divine origin, not a single letter or punctuation mark could be changed.

The Quran was revealed to Muhammad in sections over a period of twenty-two years. People of the time described Muhammad as experiencing a trance whenever the Quran was revealed to him. Scribes would then copy down whatever Muhammad dictated when he came out of his trance, often writing the words on pieces of stone, palm leaves, or bone. Eventually, these were collected and organized into chapters called *suras*, and copies were made.

The word *quran* means "recitation." The Quran is a book designed not to be read but rather recited as an act of worship. The Quran is the basis for Islamic religion and morality. Out of it grew the concept of the *Sharia* (literally, the path), which is Islamic law based on the Quran, and the traditions surrounding Muhammad's words and deeds (called the *Sunna*, which means "the right way"). The Sharia was intended to regulate all Muslim behavior, including

Most Muslims learn Arabic so that they can read the Quran in its original language. Some Qurans are bilingual so that the student can refer to the English whenever he or she encounters an unfamiliar word.

law, dress, diet, family life, marriage, relations between men and women, business practices, and religious rituals.

The Sunna also provides instruction for Muslims: Muhammad's actions and words serve as a model for the right way for Muslims to do things. The Sunna is recorded in a book of traditions called the *Hadith* (sayings of the Prophet). The Sunna is often used to clarify things written in the Quran. One example deals with *wudu,* or washing before prayer. The Quran requires a Muslim to wash before prayer, but it does not specify every detail. Early Muslims observed how the Prophet washed himself before he prayed and then imitated him. This practice is considered the Sunna of the Prophet.

The Quran, the Sharia, and the Sunna define the basic practices and beliefs of Islam despite some cultural and theological differences among Muslim communities. Selwaan Mahmoud, a Missouri college student, explains that all Muslims must practice the five basic tenets, or pillars, of Islam: a public declaration of faith (*shahada*), prayer, tithes (*zakat*), fasting (*saum*), and pilgrimage (*haj*). Says Selwaan: "Imagine a house supported by a pillar on each side and one in the center. The five tenets of Islam are like those pillars. If you take away one of them, the house will collapse."

Prayer is the second pillar of Islam. To nineteen-year-old Qurat Mir, it is one of the most beautiful parts of the religion:

Almost all my prayers are filled with deep emotion. Prayer gives me a feeling of gladness and peace. I welcome the chance to communicate with him who made me and the good things he has given me. I praise God for the opportunity to live in this country as opposed to other countries. It means a great deal for me to be here. Sometimes, I find myself crying because I feel bad for those who are being oppressed.

Mazien Mokhtar did not consider himself a good practicing Muslim until he was seventeen. Now prayer is central to his life. "Prayer is our link to God. In prayer, we praise him, we remember him, we ask him for guidance and give thanks to him for what he gives us, the good as well as the bad."

Muslims are required to pray five times a day: before dawn, at midday, in midafternoon, before sunset, and in midevening. If they pray in a mosque, they will be called to prayer (a ceremony called the *adhan*) by a *muezzin*. Traditionally, the muezzin stands on top of a minaret, one of the towers surrounding the mosque.

In the United States, the muezzin usually calls the congregation to prayer from inside the mosque. Five times a day, he chants:

God is great.
God is great.
I witness there is no God but God.
I witness that Muhammad is the prophet of God.
Rise to prayer.
Rise to felicity.
God is great.
God is great.
There is no God but God.

Except for Friday midday prayer, Muslims are not required to pray in a mosque. Some do, but many will pray at work, at home, on the street, in school—wherever they happen to be at the time of prayer. Inayit, whose family is Palestinian, remembers when she was a high school student and had to struggle for the right to pray during school hours:

My cousin and I were the only two Muslims in the school, and the school did not want to give us permission to leave the room to pray. Some schools set aside an empty classroom for Muslims so they can go there when it's time for prayer. Our school wouldn't at first. I told my teacher that if he wouldn't let me pray, I was going to walk out of class and do so anyway. Finally, they backed down and let us go.

As noted earlier, worshipers must perform wudu, ritual washings of the face, hands, and feet, before praying. Muslims believe that worshipers should be clean when praying to Allah.

Women pray in a separate section from men and must be covered when they are there.

When Muslims pray, they face toward Mecca, the holy city in which the *ka'bah* is located. The ka'bah is a large building inside of which there is an ancient black stone. Muslims believe it was on this site that the prophet Abraham and his son, Ishmael, built their house in ancient times.

During prayer, Muslims recite certain passages from the Quran along with material concerning the life and deeds of the prophet Muhammad. Many Muslims have memorized the complete Quran. The prayers are accompanied by a specific number of bowings, kneelings, and prostrations. One recitation in all prayers is the *Fatiha*, the first chapter of the Quran, which reads, in part, as follows:

> Praise belongs to God, Lord of the Worlds,
> The Compassionate, the Merciful
> King of the Day of Judgment
> Tis Thee we worship and Thee we ask for help
> Guide us on the straight path
> The path of those whom Thou has favored
> Not the path of those who incur Thine anger
> Nor of those who go astray.

At the completion of the last prayer, the worshipers affirm their beliefs in the oneness of Allah and in Muhammad as his prophet and then look over first their right shoulder and then their left, saying each time they look, "Peace be on you and the mercy of Allah." This is similar to the Christian practice of shaking hands and saying, "Peace be with you."

While it is permissible for Muslims to pray in a foreign language, they are encouraged to learn Arabic in order to say the prayers in the language in which the Quran was originally revealed to Muhammad.

Most Muslims feel learning Arabic is an essential part of their religion. Ibrahim Sidicki says that all thirteen of his grandfather's children were learning Arabic by the time they were seven and that "the older generation spent a lot more time on religious matters than our generation. We have so many other things to do—work, go to school—that we can't always follow their traditions. There are many young people today who can read the Quran only in English."

Prayer may be led by an imam to keep the congregation in harmony during the service. The imam is not a priest but more of a spiritual leader. He is very knowledgeable about the Quran and Islamic law. On Fridays, the imam delivers a sermon, usually based on a passage from the Quran, just as a minister uses a passage from the Bible for his or her sermon on Sunday.

During prayer, men and women sit in separate sections in the mosque. This tradition dates to the Prophet and is referred to in the Quran. Muslims explain that by sitting apart, the sexes are not tempted to think about each other while praying. Non-Muslims often view this practice as sexist, but this opinion is not

In keeping with tradition, Muslims remove their shoes as a sign of respect for Allah before praying in a mosque.

generally shared by Muslim men or women. One man explains: "When I pray to Allah, I want to be completely focused on him. I do not want to be distracted. If a woman is seated next to me, I might think of her during prayer. It shouldn't happen, but it does. You don't always have the control over your thoughts as you would like to have."

Selwaan Mahmoud thinks that the separation of the sexes is good for both men and women: "When I am in the mosque seated among women, I feel more comfortable than if I were seated next to a man. It can be distracting, and I don't want to be distracted or cause anybody else to be distracted."

Some Muslim women in America do not feel this way, however. Anna, a computer programmer who does not dress like most Muslim women, says that she believes that the separation is discriminatory: "I pray five times a day like a Muslim should, but I never pray in the mosque and I won't until men and women pray together. If men have sexual thoughts about women in the mosque, it's their problem and they will have to answer to God for it."

Throughout the Muslim world, public services (jumma) are held Friday afternoon in mosques. Most men are required to attend Friday services, although women may pray at home.

The mosque is one of the unique architectural creations of Islam. The traditional mosque consists of a prayer hall and an open courtyard where people can rest and relax. The courtyard is surrounded by walls. At each corner is a minaret or tower.

Before entering the prayer hall, Muslims are required to remove their shoes as a sign of respect to Allah. There are fountains located outside the prayer room for people to wash. In the prayer hall there is a niche in the wall called a *mihrab* that marks the direction toward which the congregation faces during prayer and which is facing in the direction of Mecca. By lining up with the mihrab, Muslims are assured of facing in the right direction for prayer. Near the mihrab stands the imam, who leads the prayer and who will usually give a sermon on Friday standing in a minbar, or pulpit, which is located near the mihrab.

In the United States, most mosques are not built in the traditional Middle Eastern way. Few have courtyards. Many mosques are lofts, apartments, storefronts, and buildings that have been adapted as a place of prayer. The physical appearance of the mosque is far less significant than its spiritual meaning.

After shahada and prayer comes the tradition of tithes, called zakat—the third pillar of Islam. Muslims are required to contribute approximately 2.5 percent of their salary to Islamic charitable institutions or the needy. Since many students are not wage earners, they are not yet expected to pay zakat. They do, however, perform charitable deeds (sadiqa). Arshia Papa is a Kansas high school senior who spends part of her time working with a youth group of Muslim teenagers in soup kitchens, retirement homes, and hospitals:

> Our youth group, which is mostly girls, visits these places and helps people. Many of them are very lonely, and they enjoy and appreciate having someone to talk to. Since many of them have never met Muslims before, we talk to them about our religion and tell them what we believe and why we dress the way we do. People often talk about what they should do to help others, but never do anything. It makes us feel good to do something.

Arshia has noticed that there is a major difference between Muslims and non-Muslims in her class regarding volunteer work:

Charity is an essential part of Muslim practice. Here a Muslim volunteer group distributes food and clothing to the homeless.

"There are others in the class who do these things to get credit so it will look good on their records for college. It's not the same feeling for us. We don't want any rewards on this earth. We do this for God's sake, because he wants us to."

Fasting, the fourth pillar of Islam, is another major obligation. Every Muslim, except children, travelers, and those who are sick, is called upon to fast from dawn to sunset during Ramadan, the holiest time of the year. Ramadan commemorates the time when Allah gave the Quran to the angel Gabriel to reveal it to Muhammad. During the fast, which lasts one month, no Muslim may eat, smoke, drink, or have sexual relations.

Fasting during Ramadan is such an important part of a Muslim's life that many individuals who stop practicing their religion still observe the practice. As one young woman explains:

*I continued to fast even though I had stopped praying and stopped
going to the mosque. Fasting was such a part of me that it was
almost impossible to give it up. When people saw that I wasn't
eating lunch, they would ask me why and I'd say, "Oh, I'm diet-
ing." But the truth was that it was a part of my religion that I
wouldn't let go.*

The last pillar of Islam is haj (pilgrimage). Muslims are expected to make a pilgrimage to Mecca at least once in their life-
time, if they are physically and financially able. The journey must
take place after Ramadan. Haj commemorates the time when
Abraham was tested by God's command that he sacrifice his only
son, who Muslims believe was Ishmael. At the last minute, God
sent a ram to be used as a substitute for the child.

When pilgrims approach the holy city, they all dress in white
robes so that everyone is equal in the sight of Allah and there is
no distinction by wealth, class, or race. In Mecca, they participate in many religious ceremonies, some of which are at the
ka'bah. The cities of Medina and Mecca are considered so sacred
that only Muslims are allowed to visit them.

While the haj takes place once a year, Muslims make personal visits to the holy city throughout the year and carry out
many of the ceremonies associated with the haj. This visitation
is called *umrah*. Umrah does not have the same religious signifi-
cance as the haj and does not relieve visitors of their responsibility to eventually make a pilgrimage.

Visiting Mecca often has a profound effect on young people.
Ibrahim Sidicki recalls the trip he made when he was eighteen
years old:

It was absolutely awesome. I don't know what I expected. I guess I thought I was going on a vacation. But when I saw the ka'bah, I was totally awed. To see what you've heard about all your life. And to see all the people there. I couldn't believe that people who were selling gold and silver would leave their merchandise unattended when called to prayer—and nobody would think of touching them.

Qurat Mir was in her early teens when she made umrah:

For me it was an end point and beginning. It was a culmination of all the things I had heard about since childhood. Seeing where it all came from. Not only the places where the Prophet was but praying together with hundreds and thousands of people from all walks of life and all cultures. It made me more spiritual. It made Islam more tangible for me.

In addition to practicing the five pillars, Muslims have other beliefs that are similar to those of Christians and Jews. Like Christians and Jews, Muslims believe in Judgment Day, the time when the heavens will open and the mountains crumble to dust. Allah will then raise the dead from their graves and judge them according to their actions and deeds. Those found guilty of sinning against God will be condemned to the pits of hell (*Jahannan*), where they will be tortured throughout eternity with jets of molten bronze, fire, bitter fruit, and foul water. The blessed receive rewards in paradise (*Jannah*), where they will experience the joy of being in the presence of Allah and his angels, and fine clothes, foods, and wine.

Both men and women will be physically and spiritually perfect and enjoy each other's company. While some Muslim men give this a sexual interpretation, the Quran does not.

There are two major divisions within Islam. Over 95 percent of Muslims are Sunnis, meaning they follow the Sunna (deeds) of the Prophet. The second major group is called Shiites, which means partisans of Ali bin Abi Taleb, the nephew of Muhammad. They believe that Ali should have been the first caliph, or commander of the faithful. Shiites also believe that there is a hidden imam, called the Mahdi, who will one day appear and bring justice to the world. Within these two groups, a number of subgroups exist. Sometimes, there are religious conflicts between Shiites and Sunnis, but each considers the other an orthodox Muslim community. In the United States, members of both groups usually worship at the same mosque.

Abdullah Brown was raised in an Anglo-Saxon Protestant household, but had serious doubts about God and religion. Growing up on army bases for most of his life, he and his family moved to Mississippi. It was a turning point in his life. Shocked by the intense racism he saw, he began to explore African-American history, focusing on black resistance. He read about Martin Luther King, Marcus Garvey, the Black Panthers, the Nation of Islam and read the autobiography of Malcolm X. He says,

> When I read Malcolm, I was impressed by the way he spoke out against falsehood and stood up and condemned injustice. Martin Luther King said, "We shall overcome someday." Malcolm said, "We shall overcome now!" I wondered what his ideology was. I wanted to learn what had transformed him and made him the great man he was. I began to study Islam. I saw what the Quran described

was reality. It described the world. This is the way that people should be living their lives, and I began to believe the Quranic description of the world was reality. I became impressed with the harmony that it brings to mankind and the justice it seeks to establish in society. Who was I to turn my back on reality?

I had Muslim friends at this time. I was impressed by their characters. They were striving to really live up to their beliefs. They were kind, generous, very God-conscious people. Even though I had not yet converted to Islam, I began to say the prayers. I had a friend from Kuwait. He called me late one night and seemed disturbed. He said that he had been talking about me to his imam and the imam told him that if I died that night, I would die a kafir *[literally, one who rejects God]. I thought about that and I decided that I didn't want that to happen. So the next day, I went to the mosque, said the* shahada, *and became a Muslim.*

The son of Christian fundamentalists, Daoud Zwink grew up in a small town in Kansas. He served in the Peace Corps in Somalia, where he met and married a Somalian woman and converted to Islam. "My parents are disappointed," he says today. "They're good people, and I tell them that so much of what I am in Islam is a reflection of what they gave me as a Christian. Islam completes my faith as a Christian."

Until recently, it was unusual for Americans outside the black community to convert to Islam unless they married a Muslim. However, in recent years, a small but growing number of white and Hispanic Americans have converted on their own.

Jean El-Ghussein, who is married to a Palestinian, converted to Islam before she met her husband. She was a student in college when she began to feel uneasy about her Christian faith:

I had been raised a Baptist and had attended a Southern Baptist college in Oklahoma. I believed in God, but I was troubled by Christ's divinity. I was always interested in religions, and I began to study Islam. It seemed more natural to me and more certain. When I decided to convert, my family was upset, of course. My grand-mother said to me, "Oh, Jean, people will never see your beautiful hair again." They knew that if they fought me, they'd be losing a daughter. So we don't talk about it [my religion]. I live it with my husband and children, I practice it, but I don't discuss it with my parents.

Jeff, like Jean, always considered himself a religious person. But when he entered college, he also felt unsatisfied with his beliefs:

I had been raised a strict Protestant, but I had a lot of problems with the religion. It bothered me to see so many people who said they believed in God and then went and did so many ungodly things. I felt myself outside my religion when I wanted to be inside. Christian-ity didn't make me feel that way. I felt spiritually empty.

Jeff had observed Muslims praying on campus and even in the dormitory in which he lived. His first reaction to them had been one of mild amusement mixed with a slight contempt. He recalls that

It seemed like a religion of foreigners. . . . I was very prejudiced against it. But I began to get in discussions about religion with Muslims, and I started to think, "Hey, this isn't as weird as I thought it was." I began to study it. It made a lot of sense to me, and it had

a lot of connections to Christianity and Judaism. That made me feel comfortable. Muslims accepted Christ as a prophet of God, not as God's Son. They accepted the Old Testament prophets. Most of what I had studied in the Bible I found in Islam. My parents were really unhappy. I don't think they've forgiven me yet.

For Anjum Mir, a student, the beauty of Islam is that it unites people of all nations, whatever their differences.

Islam is a total way of life. We are all human beings who have been created by one God. And we are here on earth for a period. We are tried here by our good deeds and bad deeds. And we will go back again to the same God. It is as simple as that. We must get guidance, or what we do and do not do, from the Holy Quran. So when I stand before God, I can say this is the book I practiced and this is the model I followed.

3.

Born in the U.S.A.

Mary Lahaj loved everything about America, its music, its culture, its parties, and the freedom to date interesting and attractive young men. Although her family were Muslims from Lebanon, Mary, like other members of her family, did not practice their faith. The only exception was that she kept a few dietary laws and fasted during Ramadan.

"By the time I was fifteen, I was socialized to American culture," Mary recalls, and she was especially proud to have made the cheerleading squad. But "I felt isolated. I felt alone. I didn't know how to pray, so I couldn't commune with God about this. Inside my house it was an invisible culture, an invisible religion. Outside was everything for me."

Mary attended an American college in Massachusetts. By the time she graduated in 1970, she no longer fasted. She had become a folksinger and joined the counterculture that was protesting against the war in Vietnam and for civil rights in the South. But as the seventies progressed, she became, in her words, "a slave to society":

Whatever society's values were, they were my values. Whatever the morals were, they were my morals. I was a slave to Madison Avenue, to the fashion industry, to the entertainment industry. I believed in romance and love. I bought everything hook, line, and sinker. I had no idea there was anything wrong with it. . . . I was enslaved, just beaten down to the ground.

In 1978, Mary Lahaj went to see a movie called *Al-rasul (The Message)*. It was a movie about the birth of Islam. It was the beginning of her road to becoming what she calls "a born-again Muslim." She began to study the way Muhammad behaved and acted during his life. Mary became a practicing Muslim. She prayed, fasted, gave charity, and covered her head, even though her brothers and her mother disagreed with these practices. Why did Mary embrace Islam so wholeheartedly? She says: "I felt that I was embracing something that hadn't been tainted by our culture. Everything there had been the same for 1,400 years. I was looking for purpose and structure and meaning, and I found it."

Today, young Muslims growing up in America are very much aware that this country offers many pleasures forbidden to Muslims. They live in a pop culture that publicly glorifies sexuality through advertising images, fashions, and music. Celebrities like Madonna, Marky Mark, and Flavor Flav are envied and imitated by millions of teenagers. Young Muslims are exposed to some classmates who take drugs, drink alcohol, smoke cigarettes, are sexually active, practice birth control, and have abortions. Muslim teenagers must make decisions in these areas just as any other teenager.

Muslim students not only have to wrestle with temptations but must often deal with intense peer pressure. For some young men and women, the fact of being different does put pressure on them to be more like others. In this respect, Muslim boys have an easier time than girls, for there is little to distinguish them from non-Muslim teenagers. They dress like the other kids, and even if they wear a *kufi* (a small cap), their peers consider it a fashion statement. They play baseball, roller-blade, and go to McDonald's. Young women, on the other hand, stand out because of their dress. By the time they reach high school, and sometimes before, most Muslim girls dress according to the accepted standards of feminine modesty as set down in the Quran. This means that they wear loose-fitting clothes with long sleeves and cover their hair with a scarf called a *hejab*.

For many young women, wearing the hejab is a fulfillment of their Muslim identity. For others, it is a burden. One young woman explains: "I wear the hejab, but I wish sometimes I didn't.

*M*ost Muslim teenage boys dress like any other American teenager.

My parents don't understand the pressure you're under when you're in a minority and are expected to bow down to the majority. It's hard to tell your parents they are wrong when they insist on something. They don't know what goes on in our school."

Not all American Muslim women, however, feel that they must dress according to what some call "ancient codes." Hatem, an African-American student at Howard University, does not cover her head or pray five times a day. In her mind, she is a "good Muslim," although many Muslims would not consider her so. For Summiyah Ahmed, whose father is Palestinian and a strict Muslim, parental pressure has made Islam a problem. She attends a Muslim school where she wears long dresses, covers her head, and sits separately from boys. Outside of school, she tries to find a balance between being an American and being a Muslim:

> *To tell you the truth, I don't wear my hejab outside of school. I don't feel comfortable with it. My really good friends aren't Muslim, and even though it's cool with them if I wear it, I really don't want to. I don't do anything that I'm not supposed to, like drink or smoke or meet boys. But I have been tempted to try.*

What sometimes makes the life of Muslim students in public schools even more difficult is that their religion forbids them to participate in what other students consider harmless fun. Non-Muslim students are often astonished to discover that a seventeen-year-old Muslim of either sex may be forbidden or refuse to "hang out" at a mall. Or that a Muslim will not go to a party where members of the opposite sex are present or alcohol is served. Tehani El-Ghussein, daughter of a Palestinian father and American mother, remembers how she felt when her parents re-

The Quran requires that Muslim girls and women cover their heads.

fused to let her visit the mall with some of her girlfriends. Tehani complained that they were treating her like an infant:

> It wasn't a big deal, really. I didn't want to do anything at the mall. I wasn't planning to secretly meet a guy or even talk to boys. It was more that I felt embarrassed to tell my girlfriends that I couldn't go. I felt a tremendous pressure to be like everybody else. They'd say, "Come on, let's go to the mall." I'd have to make up some excuse. I'd say, "My parents don't want me to go." Or I'd tell them I was busy or baby-sitting. I was not yet at the point where I could tell them, "No, my religion doesn't let me."

Muhammad Wasi, a student, is quick to point out that Islam does not forbid young Muslims to hang out at the mall. He and his Muslim friends have done so many times. But he admits that it is always easier for boys than girls:

> *There's nothing in the Quran that prevents a young person from going with friends to a mall or a movie or a walk in the park. More often the reason a parent will forbid a daughter to do these things is for cultural reasons rather than religious. Some parents feel it a disgrace if their daughter is seen in public just "hanging out." They are expressing their cultural values when they say that. They feel that by forbidding their daughter to do that, they are protecting her. However, few parents would question their sons' going to the mall. You leave the house and you say, "I'm leaving, going to mall." You might not have any purpose for going. Then your sister says, "How come he can go and I can't? It's not fair."*

Aisha Ashraf, a Muslim student from California, thinks that part of the problem is cultural: "My parents, they don't understand what it's like to be young in America. They are like a lot of people from other countries who deny they are American. . . . When I wanted to go to a movie with my girlfriend, my father said, 'What are you doing? You're twelve years old. . . . You don't do those things until you're thirty.' "

Kamal Mohammed says that there's always conflict and that how you deal with it "depends on the way you're raised. . . . In some families, there are always arguments around the mall or over the movies you see." Kamal's father notes that young people sometimes forget that "if they do not carry themselves as good Muslims, they will give Islam a worse name than it already has."

For many Muslim teenagers, the behavior of other students does sometimes present both a temptation and a problem. Khabira Abdul-Fattaah, an African-American teenager who was raised a Muslim, found herself attracted to what she calls "the dark side." After attending a Muslim private school until the eighth grade, Khabira transferred to public school. She recalls her feelings at the time: "When you go to public school from a Muslim school, you're scared. You're scared no one will like you. That you won't do well. You want to be accepted and liked." Throughout high school, Khabira had no problems with school-work or with her conduct in school. But she was drawn to people whose values were different from hers. Khabira's parents understood this attraction. They had converted to Islam before she was born. They told her that they had been in darkness and came to the light through Islam but that her experience was the reverse. Khabira elaborates:

> I was born in the light. But I saw the darkness, and I was curious about it. I began to hang out with people who were not good for a Muslim to be associated with. They smoke. They drank. They partied. What helped me was my parents' patience. They trusted me and felt that I would do what was right. That made it easy for me to finally realize how beautiful Islam was for me.

Because Islam forbids dating and physical contact between young men and women before marriage, Muslim teenagers are left out of a major part of teenage social life. Daoud Ahmed says that it's hard when you're a teenager and are naturally attracted to the opposite sex:

> When you know some of your friends are having sexual contact, and you are forbidden to be alone with a girl or have any physical

contact with her, sometimes your hormones go into overdrive. You want to be part of that life. You'd like to dance with a girl or hold her hand or put your arm around her, but your beliefs hold you back. Your mind tells you, you're lucky because your religion keeps you out of trouble. But sometimes your heart doesn't want to listen to your mind.

Tehani finds it sometimes takes a great deal of willpower to resist even the simplest temptations when others around her are enjoying themselves:

You have to make a conscious decision to do something. You have tell yourself, "No, I won't do that." If I feel that I want to pat a guy on the back, but you know you aren't supposed to have physical contact with him, you do feel frustrated at times. Prayer helps. I say, "Please, Allah, help me be patient." I know that my life is better because I don't date. Everything I do protects me. I see girls around me who get pregnant or have abortions or get diseases, and I know none of that will happen to me. I can focus on the things that I need to focus on. My studies, getting into college, having a career.

Monifa, whose father and stepmother were Muslims, hated to wear the hejab at school. So she resorted to a little deception:

As soon as I left the house, I would take it off and show my hair. I had such pretty hair, and I liked to show it off. I wanted the boys to see me. I was really crazy about boys. I would leave the house wearing loose-fitting clothes but carrying something sexy to change into when I got to school. Then, when I returned home, I would change before I entered the house back into my Muslim clothes.

Tehani El-Ghussein (upper right) is an American-born Muslim whose mother (lower right) is an American convert to Islam and whose father is Palestinian.

Torn by the conflict, Monifa left her father and stepmother and went to live with her mother, a non-Muslim who was very permissive. Monifa led a very non-Muslim life, eventually living with her boyfriend. But a fight with another girl landed her in trouble with the law and made her reexamine her own life. It eventually led her back to Islam. She prayed for forgiveness and returned to wearing head covering and loose clothes. "No one is telling me what I have to wear," she says today. "It's up to me. Before, I was a Muslim because my parents wanted me to. Now, I'm a Muslim because I want to."

For male students, the temptation to date can be stronger because they can get away with it more easily even though Islam forbids men and women to date. Joshua Burt found that he was able to manage going through high school without dating

There is no set age at which a Muslim girl or young woman is required to cover her hair. Some wait until they are in junior high or high school, others start younger.

but admitted having problems when he got to college: "It's tempting in college to date . . . it's very tempting. I went to a couple of parties the first year. I was on my own for the first time. I really had to work on myself. Islam does not permit a double standard. The same rules apply to men and women. A Muslim man who dates is committing a sin equally with a woman who does, no matter even if the society is far more permissive toward men than women."

Most Muslims either accept the restrictions or stop practicing Islam. A few try to have the best of both worlds. Deena, whose parents are Lebanese, did have a boyfriend throughout high school. But, as she recalls:

It was very hard to live a double life. My boyfriend was a star athlete and very popular, and I am a Muslim and not allowed to date. But we fell in love. We used to sneak off to see each other. We could never go anywhere because if anyone saw me, they'd tell my father. I'm Lebanese, and he was African-American and a Christian. My family might have disowned me if they found out. We never were completely intimate, but we did kiss and hold each other. It was so hard. I was hurt when he had to date other girls so that people wouldn't be suspicious of us. It was an impossible situation. I still love him, but I'm glad I went away to college and don't have to see him every day.

Although Muslim teenagers may have problems living in a society whose values are different from theirs, most adjust to American life. Their religious orientation enables them to deal with and overcome temptations. Rania Lawendy, a college student, expresses the feelings of many young Muslims:

Islam prepares you to deal with the world. Muslims who can't cope with it usually stray away. But a good Muslim can put things in focus. People ask me wouldn't you really [like to] live like Madonna? Or wouldn't you [like to] live like a rap star? My answer is no. Muslims don't envy Madonna or rock stars their money or their fame. They can't take those things to the grave with them. They can only take their good deeds and their bad deeds.

4.

High School: The Bad and the Good

The rumor had spread around the school since Tuesday. A Muslim girl, no one knew who, had been walking home from school when a car suddenly pulled alongside her. A male student she didn't know jumped out and ripped the scarf off her head, blew his nose in it, threw it back at her, jumped back in the car, and drove off, leaving the poor girl in tears.

The problem was that nobody knew if the story was true. Anam, whose family had come to America from Pakistan, felt that even if it wasn't true, it could have been. The World Trade Center in New York had recently been bombed. People had been killed in the explosion and "Muslim fundamentalists" had been arrested and charged. The air was tense and Anam could sense that when people looked at her, their looks were not friendly. And so she made a major decision:

As a Muslim woman, I am required to cover my hair. We do this to avoid attracting men and engaging in flirtations. It is a way of protecting us. In my parents' country, all women are covered, so none

of us stand out. But in America, being covered makes you stand out.
I am a very religious person, but I do not want to draw attention to
myself. So I decided not to wear my hejab in public.

Anam's problem is one that is shared by many young Muslim
women. While their religion requires them to be covered, they
feel they need to make compromises for reasons of personal
safety.

Although Muslim students are not usually bothered in school,
harassment can suddenly escalate in times of crisis. Several Muslim students in southern high schools were slammed against
lockers and walls during the Gulf War. Sadeck, a ninth-grade
student in New Jersey, remembers how painful it was for her to
go to public shool after the World Trade Center bombing. "The
kids would call me towel-head," she says, "and threaten to remove my hejab to see if I was bald."

In Washington, D.C., two young Muslim women were
bumped by a man who deliberately crossed the street to walk
into them. In Michigan, a female student tried to pull a hejab off
the head of a Muslim student and discovered, to her astonish-
ment, that Muslim women are not necessarily pacifists. "She
didn't mess with me anymore after that," the Muslim student recalls, adding, "We are taught to avoid fighting if we can, but if
we can't, then we should avoid losing."

Most Muslim students learn to handle the petty annoyances
from other students without too much difficulty if the behavior
is childish and not vicious. Muhammad Jihad, a student in Ohio,
says that after a bomb exploded on a Pan Am jet over Scotland,
killing everyone on board, a fellow student asked him if he was
the guy who planted the bomb. "It was a stupid thing to say, and

I felt as bad as anybody. In fact, I think I felt a lot worse than most." Another student says that when she first entered high school and wore a hejab, some students spread a rumor that she was receiving chemotherapy for cancer and that she covered her head because she had lost all her hair. "It was dumb, but that's the kind of thing you have to put up with if you're a Muslim." Tehani El-Ghussein recalls that she was friendly with a Jewish student who sat behind her in class: "I hadn't covered when I first was in class, so he didn't know I was Muslim. Then, when I decided to cover, he was shocked. He asked me if I was Muslim, and I said yes. 'Aren't we supposed to hate each other?' he said. He was kind of kidding, and we were friendly afterwards, but it was never the same."

Some students have problems with their teachers. A few

The tenets of a Muslim religious school written on the T-shirt of a student.

teachers are openly hostile to Muslims. One student remembers how a teacher once remarked, "Your people are enemies of the United States." Other teachers, while not expressing their hostility openly, do so in subtle ways. Deena, who eventually left public school to attend a Muslim school, was denied permission to take advanced courses even though her grades made her eligible. "My teacher never said why he denied me," she says, "but I was sure that it was because of my religion."

Malal Omar, an honor student and an excellent basketball player, remembers how she and her friend Inayet had to overcome their coach's prejudices:

> We were both good enough to be starters. But we did not wear the usual basketball shorts and short sleeves that the other players wore because we are Muslims. Instead we kept our head covered and wore loose clothing when we played. Our coach, who was male, didn't understand this. When we went out on the court he said, "Come to the sidelines, what are you doing there?" At first he didn't play us. He kept us on [the] bench for a while, which was a downer, a blow to our egos . . . but when he saw that our dress didn't interfere with our playing, he was cool.

Some teachers perpetuate the stereotypes that all Muslims are rich oil sheiks and terrorists. Other teachers who discuss Islam or the Middle East in class often get the facts wrong. One student recalls sitting in class listening to the teacher giving incorrect information about Arab history: "I wasn't strong enough to speak out. So I sat there listening to all those distortions, burning inside." Another Muslim student, Mai Abdala, took the opposite position at her school: "When a teacher made a mistake, I spoke up—and said too much." Another student reports: "I had a teacher who called my religion Mohammedanism. I corrected him, and he got angry. He showed me a book in which the term was used. I said, 'Yes, but this book was written by a Western man a long time ago who didn't understand us. We don't worship Muhammad. He was a prophet, not a God. It offends us when somebody calls us Mohammadans.' The teacher accepted the criticism, but he wasn't happy about it. I had to work real hard to keep my A in his class."

Far more difficult to deal with are the teachers who sometimes try to embarrass a Muslim student or express hostility to Muslims. Most Muslim students try to explain their position in class, but by doing so they run the risk of becoming the target of

Mai Abdala is one of the few Muslim students at her high school. Despite the fact that she cannot participate in all the activities that her non-Muslim classmates do, her beliefs are respected by others.

the teacher's anger—and receiving poor grades. Selwaan Mahmoud had one teacher who she felt was hostile: "I would talk in class about Islam. Nothing political, just trying to explain the religion. Then my history teacher would say, 'Well what about Iran and Iraq?' Or he'd make a remark that women have to walk ten feet behind men. He was either ignorant or just trying to annoy me."

Many people believe that Muslim women are restricted if not oppressed by men. This is true in some countries where the patriarchal tradition is strong, modernization is limited, and religious fervor is high. Historically, Islam improved the condition of women at the time of the prophet Muhammad by guaranteeing them certain basic rights, and ending female infanticide, which some of the desert clans practiced. Today, middle-class women in most Muslim countries enjoy a wide variety of rights. (This isn't always the case for poorer women.) All of the young Muslim women interviewed for this book strongly denied they were oppressed in any way in the United States. Anjum Mir remarked: "People are very appearance-oriented. They don't understand it. They have to be educated. We don't feel subjugated. Separation makes us feel more equal. We feel men respect us as a person, not as a sexual object."

Qurat Mir gets annoyed when people judge her and her friends on the basis of her appearance and stereotypical notions:

> Just because we are covered and don't date and sit separately from men in the mosque or in class, people say we are oppressed. That's just not so. Just because a woman wears sexy clothing, does that make her free spirited? Just because we wear loose clothes and are covered, does that make us oppressed and sedated? The only true

freedom for me is freedom of the mind. Not being trapped by your body frees the mind. By being covered the mind shows. People deal with you for what you are, not how you look.

Rania Lawendy, a college student who is invited to high schools to speak to students about this issue, shares Qurat's feelings:

I don't feel Western women are free. Muslim women had the right to have property and vote long before Western women could. When a woman's money was her husband's in the West, Muslim women kept whatever they earned. I don't think it's freedom to show off your body. American women need to be educated. No one can tell me that they're more free than I am!

Another problem Muslim students have to contend with is charges of terrorism. Whenever there is a violent incident, some Muslims become tense. They try to explain to other students that the terrorism has nothing to do with them. Ibrahim Sidicki, a college student, has spoken to many students:

I try to tell them that the overwhelming majority of Muslims living in the United States are Americans and America is now their country. Whatever people do to hurt this country, hurts us as well. Secondly, I say to judge us by the actions of a few terrorists is like us judging you on the basis of a few mass killers. We know serial killers exist in this country, but we don't look at all Americans as serial killers. So don't look at all of us as terrorists.

Homosexuality is another issue that often leads to some spirited debates with non-Muslims. Nizar Muhammed says that

Muslims consider homosexuality to be a sin and as going against the natural order. He quotes the passages in the Quran in which Allah says the prophet Lot chastised his people: "Do you commit lewdness such as no people in creation ever committed before you? For you practice your lusts on men in preference to women: you are indeed transgressing beyond bounds" (7:80–81). According to the Quran, one of the main reasons God destroyed Sodom was homosexual activity. Muslims believe the purpose of sexual relations is to have children.

Even though their beliefs and behavior are different from those of non-Muslims, and despite the occasional problems that arise, Muslim students, for the most part, enjoy public school and make good friends there. Ayesha Kezmi recalls that her non-Muslim friends helped her assert her identity as a Muslim: "I did not cover my head until I was in high school. Although I felt myself a sincere Muslim, I did wonder about the kind of life other students were living. Interestingly, it was my non-Muslim friends who encouraged me to assert my identity as a Muslim. I strongly believe that you can't stay to yourself. You have to have both non-Muslim and Muslim friends."

Some students believe that their friends show them more respect because they're Muslim. Joshua Burt notices how his friends' behavior has changed: "If they cuss, they apologize right away. I like that because it shows respect for me. They're sorry almost before it comes out of their mouth. So it helps them. They don't cuss so much. I also notice that they also drink less. If we're out together, they may drink a Coke instead of a beer because they know my religion forbids alcohol." Rania was elected senior class president in her high school even though there were no other Muslim students in attendance. "I feel they elected

In some of her courses dealing with world history, Mai Abdala is able to correct any students' misconceptions about Islam.

me," says Rania, "because they know that as a Muslim, I don't lie, I don't cheat, and I can be trusted to keep my word." She finds that her girlfriends trust her with their secrets and talk to her about their fears: "Because I'm a Muslim, they know I won't try and steal their boyfriends and I could look at things objectively and tell them the truth." Kalil says that his classmates even help him to be a better Muslim: "I notice that during Ramadan, they try and help me keep my fast. They don't eat around me, and some of them even try to fast with me for a day or two. They try to keep me in check." Tehani El-Ghussein remembers that when she was about to enter high school, she felt a great deal of anxiety about covering her head. Her best friend, who was not Muslim, said, "Hey, do it! That's your religion. It's cool."

Some Muslim students find that practicing Islam in a non-Muslim country is hard. Anjum Mir notes that "America is the best place to practice Islam. You have a freedom here that you won't find in many places. But to be a Muslim in America, you need support. It's very difficult if you're alone. You need to practice with others."

Muslim students often think that they must act as a model for others. As one teenage girl put it: "If you do not carry yourself as a good Muslim, you give Islam a bad name. When people see how I act, they see I have a moral code. I once found $100, and I returned it. Some of the kids thought I was crazy. Then I heard someone say, 'Oh, she's a Muslim.' What that means to me is that I fear God."

Sometimes, Muslim students feel a certain degree of alienation from non-Muslim students, who are much less serious than they are. Qurat Mir found many of her fellow high school students to be "hollow. I really saw people around me only concerned with petty things, how they looked, about their dates, things like that. It bore no relevance to the kind of life I wanted for myself."

To give their children a fuller religious life and to avoid exposing them to the problems and temptations in public school, some Muslims send their children to a religious school rather than a public school. Throughout the United States there are only 165 full-time Muslim schools, and many of them go only as high as the eighth grade. As a result, only one of every ten Muslim children attends a Muslim school. While elementary school children are sent by their parents, some Muslim high school students ask to switch from public school to Islamic school.

For Raisa, an eighth-grade student at an Islamic school, her choice of school was based on fear: "I was afraid to go to public school. Sometimes, it was dangerous. People got robbed and beaten. I felt I would be much safer in a Muslim school." Nadia, whose family comes from Turkey, hated her public school: "Nobody bothered me or anything like that. But it was hard practicing my religion in public school. Most kids didn't understand what we did or why we did it. I didn't like the language some of the kids used, or some of the music that preached violence. I am an American but I'm also a Muslim, and I want to be a good Muslim and a good American. In a Muslim school, I can be both."

Tariffa, a sophomore in an Islamic school in Ohio, voluntarily transferred from a public school to a Muslim school to avoid personal problems. She was aware that she was headed for serious trouble unless she changed her lifestyle:

> *I was already getting in trouble in intermediate school. I was sneaking out for dates. I would try a drink once in a while. I liked boys and was attracted to them. I knew that if I went to high school, I would get in really serious trouble. So I asked my parents to send me to a Muslim school. Now I focus on my studies and being a good Muslim and doing something with my life.*

Young men also find Muslim schools help them avoid temptation. Thomas, who is sixteen, says that "in public schools, it seemed like everyone was into drugs, stuff like crack cocaine, reefer, booze. It was hard not to do that, especially when you were out with your buddies and everybody else was doing it. So I decided to go to a religious school."

Most of the students who attend Islamic schools feel secure in their religious beliefs. They are able to enjoy their lives as

Muslims, free from the pressures of socializing, smoking, and drinking that are found in most high schools. For Jeremy, the Muslim school offers him the chance for a better future: "In my regular high school, many kids drop out and don't go on to college. Here, just about everybody goes to college."

Muslim schools differ in many ways from the public schools. In larger schools, boys and girls are taught in separate classrooms. In smaller schools, they may sit in the same room but in separate sections. There is no socializing, which seems to bother the boys more than the girls. An eighth-grade male student says that the hardest part about being in a Muslim school "is you can't hang out with the girls."

Islamic schools, like all religious schools, must meet standards set by the state board of education. History, mathematics, sciences, and social studies are taught. But since Muslim schools are private, they are allowed to teach religion. Part of the school is used as a mosque. Arabic is a basic requirement because students are expected to eventually read the Quran in Arabic. Courses are also given in Islamic civilization.

Is there any conflict between secular education and Islamic religion? There can be, especially when dealing with the scientific explanations of how the world was created and how human beings evolved. Islam holds that God created the world and human beings. Scientific theory talks of creation and evolution as natural phenomena that can be explained without God. In Islamic schools, both views are presented. The contemporary theory of evolution is taught with the qualification that it presents what many modern scientists believe, if not what Islam believes. However, some Muslim schools tip the scales in favor of Quranic teaching and minimize other theories.

Mai does not wear shorts or take gym classes; she works out in the exercise room instead.

While in most public schools sex and drug education is an important part of the curriculum, these courses are not offered at many Muslim schools. Firky Fahny, a teacher, explains:

One reason that many schools teach sex education is that pregnancy, birth control, abortion, and diseases are problems in their schools. Here, we do not have those problems. Muslim women do not have those kind of relationships until after they are married. Nor do we have drug problems, as drugs and alcohol are forbidden by the Quran. In the Quran it is written, "O you who attain to faith; intoxicants, games of chance and idolatrous practices and divining the future are but a loathsome evil of Satan's doing. Shun them so that you might attain to a happy state." As for questions of abortion and birth control for married couples, these too are guided by Islamic

law. Some forms of birth control are permissible, but abortion is
generally forbidden, with some exceptions such as endangerment to
the mother's life.

But even though these subjects are not taught in school, most
students are knowledgeable about them. "We have families," one
freshman student says, "and we discuss these things with them."

Many non-Muslims believe that Muslim students are brain-
washed and accept the Quran without question. On the contrary,
says Kariema: "Islam is a bunch of questions. You have to know
what you are accepting. You just can't accept things without
knowing what they are. I believe Islam has an answer for every
question. But you have to find it out for yourself." Selwaan Mahmoud elaborates on what Islam has to offer:

> *It's how good you are to your brother and sister; it's how considerate*
> *you are, how much you control your temper; it's not making jokes*
> *or fun of people behind their backs. And these are things that we*
> *learned from the Prophet's Sunna and from the Quran. Whether you*
> *work or socialize with people, they know you for who you are, and*
> *Islam makes you a better person.*

Most Muslim students are comfortable with their religion and
with being Muslim in a society that is often in conflict with their
values. Suzani says, "I love Islam. Islam is a way of life, not just a
religion. It's my language, my culture, my history, my morals. I
consider myself a Muslim-American, and when people ask me
which side of the hyphen is stronger, I say, 'I love America and I
owe a lot to this country, but I am a Muslim first.' "

5.

Love and Marriage

When Yasir al-Janabi, a Muslim college student, decided he might want to court and marry a young Muslim woman who attended the same school, his first goal was to learn her name. But unlike his American friends, he could not just go up and introduce himself and invite the woman for a cup of coffee. Nor could he hope of having a romantic relationship with her. The Quran forbids any sexual relationships outside of marriage. The prophet Muhammad advised Muslims: "He who is sexually mature, let him get married. If he cannot afford to get married, let him fast to help him completely abstain [from sexual activities]."

In Muslim countries, families often arrange for young people to meet each other. In America, young Muslims tend to meet through social events and weddings in the mosque or in clubs on campus. Since Yasir belonged to several Muslim organizations on campus, he knew that it would only be a matter of time before this woman would join one of them. Once she did, he would be able to find out her name—Sana—and learn whether she had any relatives on campus.

The first time Yasir spoke to Sana was during a meeting when Muslim students were discussing organizing a demonstration on behalf of Bosnian Muslims. Yasir was impressed by her clear thinking and intelligence. They addressed each other as "brother" and "sister" so as to minimize any flirtation. The more he heard her speak, the more certain he was of his choice. When he discovered that Sana had a brother, Abdullah, on campus, Yasir decided he would meet him and cultivate his friendship.

Over the next several weeks, Yasir and Abdullah became friends. Once he felt secure in his friendship, Yasir finally revealed to Abdullah what had been in his mind all along—

At Rutgers University Muslim students meet regularly to discuss various topics, from world politics to marriage, that concern Muslims.

courtship of his sister. Abdullah, who liked Yasir, agreed to convey the message to his family. He told his parents, who in turn spoke with Sana. Sana was shocked. Although she planned to marry eventually, she was not thinking of it at this point. Her first reaction was to reject the proposal. Abdullah suggested that she at least give Yasir a chance, and she finally agreed to do so. She insisted that she had to get to know him first. He could call her on the telephone. He could visit her and her family. She would try to keep an open mind, but she wanted Yasir to know that she felt she was not yet ready to marry. Secretly, she was flattered to be asked because she liked him.

Sana's parents believed that the decision was hers to make. According to tradition, her father would have to approve her choice, if she decided she loved him and wanted to marry. While he thought that Sana should finish college before marrying, he also felt that she was mature enough to decide for herself. His main concern was that Yasir had what he called "good habits." By this he meant that Yasir was a good Muslim, who sincerely followed the teachings of Islam.

Over the next several weeks, Sana spoke to Yasir over the phone and in the Muslim groups. At the same time, her brother made discreet inquiries about him. The reports were good. He was a devout Muslim, an excellent student, and seemed to have a good future ahead of him as a chemical engineer. Early in their discussions, Sana made it clear that if she decided to marry, she wanted to complete her education and work in her chosen field of medical research. Nor did she want to have children right away. If these conditions were not acceptable to Yasir, he shouldn't waste his time. Yasir agreed to them.

An essential part of the courtship process is for the families to meet and get to know one another. Yasir explained, "This is because it is not simply two individuals who marry, but two families who will be joined." Parental permission is essential for marriage in most Muslim families. According to tradition, daughters seek permission from their fathers and sons from their mothers. Sana feels perfectly comfortable with this arrangement, even though she knows that Americans believe the decision should be the couple's: "I trust my parents. I believe that they love me and only want the best for me. They have had far more experience than I and if my father objects to someone I want to marry, I would respect his judgment. But the reasons must be good Islamic ones. He cannot reject someone because of ethnicity or skin color."

Sana has a girlfriend whose family was from Syria and who was considering as a suitor an African-American Muslim she liked very much. Her friend's father tried to block the match:

> Her father is a very successful businessman, very status conscious, and when my friend asked if this young man could visit, he said no after learning he was black. He gave all sorts of excuses. He didn't think he was a good Muslim. He wouldn't be able to support her. She answered every objection he raised. Then he said he thought it better if she married somebody from Syria, from her own culture. She told him that this was America and she wasn't going to limit herself to a narrow cultural range. Her father refused to give in and she did not go against his wishes.

Although most Muslim young women will not risk breaking up the family by refusing to accept their father's decision, some do appeal the decision to an arbitration panel. The panel is in-

Although Muslim women may be physically separated from Muslim men in the classroom, they actively participate in classroom discussions.

formal and is often made up of members of the mosque, other members of the family, and an imam. If the panel believes that the refusal is based on other than Islamic reasons — such as race—it can override the father's refusal. Usually daughters will accept their father's decision, even if they feel it is unjust. Fathers generally try to act with restraint because they know they might win the battle but lose the respect of their daughter as a result.

While men have more latitude in choosing a wife without parental approval, sons usually ask their mother's permission. Yasir says that if his mother objected, and he could not persuade her to accept his choice, he would listen to her. He says Muslims believe that " 'Paradise lies at the mother's feet.' If I refused to listen to her, I would be disrespecting her. And I could not do that."

In reality, both parents and children want to avoid conflicts over marriage. One young woman who thought she was in love said that she was angry with her father when the young man proposed and her father said no. "He told me that he had done some checking and found out that the young man did not pray, had some bad 'habits,' did not finish college, and seemed not to have a promising future. I was unhappy, but I accepted his decision because his reasons were good ones."

Sana's father says, "All I want for my daughter is to marry a man who is a good Muslim and who is honest and sincere, willing to work hard, and, I prefer, [has] a good education."

A Muslim man is free to marry a non-Muslim, but their children must be brought up Muslim. Islamic law forbids a Muslim woman to marry a non-Muslim, unless he converts. As a result, many non-Muslims who marry Muslim women superficially convert to Islam. They sometimes are called, half jokingly, half contemptuously, "cupid's Muslims."

The requirement of parental consent, while Islamic in origin, is also tied to cultural traditions. Many young people's parents or grandparents immigrated to the United States from the Middle East, Asia, or eastern Europe and have maintained many of their customs.

Most immigrants live among their own ethnic groups and try to re-create their ethnic culture in America. In their neighborhoods can be found a variety of clothing, music, and bookstores, restaurants, and groceries, that sell the products from their countries. But as their children become Americanized, parents and children sometimes find themselves in conflict.

Take Hane's parents as an example. They are from eastern Europe, are very devout, and send Hane to a Muslim school.

After class, men and women discuss issues raised in the class. They address each other as "brother" and "sister."

They insist they will play a large role in her selection of a husband. Outwardly Hane appears to conform to what is expected of her, but inwardly she is rebelling.

My father is very strict about the religion. I do a lot of things because he wants me to, but if I had my choice, I would not do them. It sounds awful, but that's the way I feel. When I get married, I don't want to have someone select my husband for me. I want to get to know him beforehand to be sure he will be kind to me. He doesn't have to be a Muslim as far as I am concerned. All he has to be is a good person. I would never tell my father this, because he would never understand. But I feel more American than Muslim. I try hard to practice Islam, but it's to please others, not myself.

Hane's friends blame her parents for turning her away from Islam. Muhammad, who is Pakistani, charges: "They haven't taught her properly. They try to force things on her. They don't explain anything." Muhammad's father agrees:

In this society I cannot force anything on my children. I can only tell them what is right and what is wrong. "This is fire, if you put your hand in it, you will get burned. You can believe me or you can try it out." . . . Some young people don't listen. They want to try it out for themselves. So there's an easy way to learn and a difficult way. It's entirely up to you. I myself have never forced anything on my children.

While the general impression is that Muslim parents are stricter in their religion than their children, sometimes the opposite is true. "My son has become an even better Muslim in many ways than I have," one father remarks. Razan's father, who is a doctor, was very proud of her beauty and was shocked when she decided to wear the hejab. Razan remembers: "My father said, 'What are you doing? You have such beautiful hair. You're only twelve years old. You don't have to do that now.' Before I covered he used to take me to dinners and show me off to his friends. After I covered he . . . stopped inviting me."

Rania Lawendy says that the key to adjustment is her family. She feels Muslim families are very solid compared to those of Americans. "We look at families of our friends at schools. They have no respect for their parents. We have good families. We are brought up to respect our parents and our brothers and sisters. I remember when a girl in my high school taught me that when she wanted her brother's jeans after he stopped wearing them, he sold them to her! I was shocked. Not me! Such a thing could not happen in our family. Because our family is strong, because we respect one another, our belief in Islam is strong. The stronger the family, the stronger the faith."

Many American students want to know why Muslim men are allowed to have as many as four wives at one time, and why divorce is far easier for a man than a woman. Muslim students explain that before Muhammad, men treated women very badly and took an unlimited number of women as wives or mistresses. Islam regulated this practice by limiting the number of wives to four. However, Muhammad recommended that a man should have only as many wives as he could afford. For most people, this meant no more than one.

Muslims also point out that polygamy is disappearing throughout the world since many Muslim women object to it. Moreover, many families cannot afford to support the large numbers of children that are produced in polygamous families. Most Muslim families who immigrated to America, where polygamy is illegal, were monogamous before they arrived.

Marriage, like everything else in the life of Muslims, is regulated by the Quran and Islamic law. Islam, like Judaism and Christianity, is patriarchal. The husband is considered the head of the household. His major responsibility is to provide for the well-being of his wife and children. The wife's major responsibility is to take care of the children. However, she is not obligated to do housework, and is free to work. Since many young married Muslim women have jobs, husbands and wives often share household responsibilities. According to the Quran, a woman is entitled to keep whatever she earns for herself if she wants.

Many Americans feel that Muslim men rule the household.

"If they mean that men do not respect the rights of their wives, that's not so," says Abdullah Brown. He points out that Allah does not want a husband to be an oppressor. He notes, "The prophet Muhammad once said to his followers, 'the best of you are those who are best to their families.' It doesn't make sense to try and dominate your wife. Each has his or her respective role. Islam teaches that the man has the final decision in the family, but you should always discuss things with your wife and try to reach a joint decision. The family is a single unit and should be harmonious."

PART II

*I*slam in the

African-American

Community

6.

Islam Comes to America

When the first Muslims from the Middle East arrived in America, they were unaware that Islam had originally been brought here from Africa as early as the seventeenth century. For almost 300 years, some ten million men, women, and children were uprooted from their homes and brought to America's shores as slaves. Perhaps as many as 20 percent of them were Muslims.

Some African Muslims wrote of their life in their native land. While most whites believed Africa was a place filled with primitive savages, men like Omar Ibn Said, who was captured in Africa and eventually gained his freedom in America, revealed his home in West Africa to be a wealthy land with a highly developed society. In 1831, after converting to Christianity, he wrote an account of his past life in Africa:

Before I came to a Christian country, my religion was the religion of Mohammed—the Apostle of God. I walked to the mosque before daybreak. I washed my face, my hands and feet. I prayed at noon,

*prayed in the afternoon, prayed at sunset, prayed at night. I gave
alms every year—gold, silver, seeds, goats. I went every year to holy
war against the infidels. I made pilgrimage to Mecca. When I left
my country, I was 37 years old. I have been in the country of the
Christians 24 years.*

As slaveowners forced slaves to abandon Islam and accept
Christianity, African-Americans lost memory of their former religion. But other forces were preparing the ground for its rebirth.
In the 1800s, black people had been so brutalized and ostracized
by whites that some began to think of returning to Africa. As
early as 1815, a free black man by the name of Paul Cuffee advocated a return-to-Africa movement and financed a small colony
in Sierra Leone. But it was not until 1851 that the separatist
movement took an Islamic turn. Eric Blyden, a brilliant scholar
born in the West Indies, left the United States and emigrated to
Liberia, where he was to remain for forty years as a teacher,
builder, and political leader. Blyden was aware that many slaves
had been Muslims who had been forced to convert to Christianity. He maintained that Islam was the natural religion for African
peoples, whereas "Christianity, which focused on denying African values, had a destructive . . . influence on Africans."

By the early 1900s, other African-American men and women
were seriously considering Islam. In 1913, a North Carolina man
by the name of Timothy Drew claimed that he had visited Morocco and had been deeply impressed with Islam. He said that
he had received a commission from the king of Morocco to teach
Islam to blacks in America. Setting up his headquarters in Newark, New Jersey, Drew took the name Noble Drew Ali. He began
to preach that true emancipation for black people would come

from knowing their heritage. He refused to call himself or his followers Negroes. According to Drew, blacks were really "Asiatics" or "Moorish," and Islam was the proper religion for the peoples of Asia while Christianity was for Europeans.

Noble Drew Ali founded the Moorish Science Temple in Newark, New Jersey, in 1913. Men dressed in red *fezzes* (Turkish hats) and wore black suits. Women wore long dresses, white on the Sabbath. Because most members did not speak Arabic and were Bible oriented, they were not orthodox Muslims. However, Noble Drew Ali did introduce the concept of Islam to the black community.

Whatever influence the Moorish Science Temple may have had in the black community, it was overshadowed by another movement that powerfully affected African-Americans after the First World War ended in 1919. Because hundreds of thousands of black men had served courageously in the army, many African-Americans hoped that blacks would now be treated with respect and justice. White America responded to these hopes with the lynch rope and the torch. Seventy blacks were lynched in 1919, eleven of them burned alive. There were twenty-five race riots throughout the country and almost 100 lynchings. In Chicago alone, thirty-eight people died.

This brutal treatment of blacks led many to respond to a new separatist movement that had taken root by the First World War. The leader of the movement was Marcus Garvey, a West Indian who had formed the Universal Negro Improvement Association, known as UNIA. UNIA's goal was to unite the black people of America. Garvey wanted to transport as many African-Americans to Africa as possible. His goal was to create a black state in Africa where all his people might live and prosper in social and legal equality.

Garvey preached racial pride. "Up you mighty race," he exhorted his people, "you can conquer what you will. Build your future on these foundations. Freedom—Justice—Equality." His motto was "One God—One Aim—One Destiny." Garvey maintained that the black man would never receive justice in America. Therefore he should leave the country that oppresses and despises him and build his own country. To finance his program, Garvey began a number of business enterprises. All failed. Eventually, he was arrested for fraud and sent to prison. Many blacks believe he was imprisoned for attempting to fight white oppression.

Garvey was not Muslim, but his doctrine of racial separatism had a powerful influence on Islamic leaders in the black community. In 1930, as the Great Depression caused tremendous suffering throughout the African-American community, a peddler appeared in Detroit who was known by several names. He called himself W. D. Fard or Fard Muhammad. Fard Muhammad said he was born in Mecca of an Arab father and a European mother and had come to America on a mission. One woman remembers: "He came first to the house selling raincoats and afterwards silks. He told us the silks he carried were the same kind that our people used in our home country, and that he was from there. So we would ask him to tell us about our home country."

Fard Muhammad began to hold meetings in people's homes. He told them that they were a people from Asia and that their natural religion was Islam. He preached a black God and a black nation. He told people that they were not "Negroes"—that was the white man's term—but black men and women. They had be-

Marcus Garvey was the first advocate of African-American nationalism who had a mass following.

come separated from their true identity and must be brought back to it. Fard said that black Americans could never achieve freedom, justice, or equality in the United States. He advocated a separate black nation where African-Americans could govern themselves. Fard named his movement "The Lost-Found Nation of Islam in the Wilderness of North America." Today, it is known as the Nation of Islam.

7.

The Nation of Islam

When Conrad Tillard was a freshman in college, he was a deeply troubled young man. His childhood had been difficult, his parents were divorced, and he was trying to come to terms with his manhood—a difficult process for many black youths in America. As Conrad explains: "I was a young black man who felt deep within myself that I had the potential to be somebody. But everywhere I went I felt the sting of racism. Then I heard this teaching. I felt that it was directed at me. I heard my feelings be expressed by someone else. It completely changed my life."

The teaching Conrad heard was that of the Nation of Islam and Minister Louis Farrakhan, the leader of the Nation. "The Nation taught me to know myself—that self-knowledge is the basis of all knowledge," says Conrad. "It taught me about my own people and my own civilization. It was the first time in my life that anyone ever told me that the condition of our people was not exclusively our fault. That no matter what my economic status is, there was tremendous value in me."

Conrad joined the Nation of Islam and took the name Conrad Muhammad. Today, he is the minister of the New York
mosque of the Nation of Islam. His major mission is to save black
people from self-destruction and from destruction by a society
that, after 400 years of slavery and segregation, continues to be
racist. What makes his task more difficult is the ongoing controversy surrounding the Nation of Islam. It is a controversy that, in
one form or another, has been raging on and off for nearly thirty-
five years.

In 1959, the Nation of Islam, then barely known outside the
black community, was the subject of a television documentary.
Produced by Mike Wallace, now the chief correspondent of the
CBS program *60 Minutes,* the show was called "The Hate that
Hate Produced." The message of the program was that the Nation of Islam was a black Muslim organization that preached hatred of whites. Malcolm X, who was then a member of the
Nation and its chief spokesman, recalled in his autobiography
the hysterical reaction of the public:

> *The title—The Hate that Hate Produced—was edited tightly in a
> kaleidoscope of shocker images. . . . Mr. [Elijah] Muhammad, me
> and others speaking . . . strong-looking, set-faced black men, our
> Fruit of Islam. . . . Every phrase was edited to increase the shock
> mood. In New York City there was an instant avalanche of public
> reaction. Hundreds of thousands of New Yorkers, white and black,
> were exclaiming, "Did you hear it? Did you see it? Preaching hate
> of white people?"*

Despite the fact that few people had heard of the Nation
of Islam until the program was broadcast, the Nation had been

preaching racial pride and attacking white racism since Fard Muhammad founded the Nation during the 1930s. An unemployed automobile worker by the name of Elijah Poole heard Fard's message and became his devoted disciple. He changed his name to Elijah Muhammad and eventually moved to Chicago, where he organized Temple Number 2 of the Nation of Islam. Fard, after some difficulty with the police, mysteriously vanished in the early 1930s. Elijah Muhammad became the leader of the Nation of Islam. He was determined to free blacks from the corrupt influence of whites and remove all traces of slavery from them. His goal was to save his people from destruction by teaching them self-pride and instilling in them the courage to stand up to racism. As he told them in a speech: "The white man, he has filled you with fear of him ever since you were little black babies. So over you is the greatest enemy a man can have—and that is fear. . . . I am going to preach to you the truth until you are free of that fear."

Elijah Muhammad continued and expanded upon the teachings of Fard Muhammad, who, he believed, was the incarnation of God. Houses of worship were called Temples of Islam. The University of Islam, which Fard Muhammad had founded for young men and women, offered courses in black history, with emphasis on black leaders. Instruction was also given in the Quran, and young women were taught home economics skills and how to be good wives and mothers. Men were recruited into the Fruit of Islam, a paramilitary organization designed to protect the organization and its leaders and to teach discipline to young men. Women wore long skirts and covered their heads. Men dressed in suits and ties. Alcohol, drugs, cigarettes, adultery, and dancing (except between husband and wife) were prohibited.

One of the most famous members of the Nation of Islam, heavyweight champion Muhammad Ali, pays tribute to the Honorable Elijah Muhammad, whose photograph appears in the background. (© Ted Gray/New York Public Library)

Monogamous relationships were encouraged, and divorce was rarely permitted.

The emphasis was on racial pride and freedom from oppression of the white man. Elijah Muhammad required members of the Nation to give up their last names, which were their slave names—every black person in America had the name of the white man who originally owned him or her—and replace it with an X. The X symbolized their unknown African name and also their unknown potential. Elijah Muhammad also provided his members with a history of the origins of black people designed to elevate them. He taught that black people were descended from the tribe of Shabbaz, which originated in Africa early in man's history. Muhammad claimed that the white man was created by an evil black scientist named Yacub, who grafted weaker black genes to create the white man. According to Elijah Muhammad, the white man was destined to rule for some 6,000 years. The arrival of W. D. Fard signaled that the time had come for the black man to assume his rightful destiny. Elijah Muhammad claimed that Fard was Allah and that he, Elijah Muhammad, was God's messenger. His mission was to form a black nation within America. "We are not and cannot be American citizens," he said, "since we are not Americans by race."

He also put great emphasis on education and set up parochial schools modeled on the University of Islam in association with the temples. Students were taught about great black Arab and African leaders such as Al-Mansur and Nyssa of Mali, conqueror of Timbuktu in Africa. They studied African-American history, language skills, art, mathematics, science, Islamic relations, Arabic, and English. Classes were held fifty weeks of the year, with no sports or free time for play, rest, or food snacks. Boys and girls were kept in separate classes. "We won't have sweethearting going on while education is supposed to be going on," Minister Louis Farrakhan, the present leader of the Nation of Islam, once remarked.

Many black parents, Muslim and non-Muslim, approved of the school and its discipline because it promoted pride in being black and gave students a sense of hope for the future. One parent commented: "I put my son in the University of Islam because it is my school. They do not teach him he is inferior to anyone else. They teach him to accept his color and be proud that he is black."

One student explained what a Nation of Islam school meant for her: "I spend more time studying, which I would not do when I was in the public schools. I cannot afford to waste my time. I want to make something out of myself, that will benefit my nation and myself."

Elijah Muhammad refused to accept not only the white man's characterizations of the black man but his religion and society as well. "The Bible is the graveyard of my people," he said. He rejected the divinity of Christ and the Christian doctrine of turning the other cheek:

> Let us use the Moslem Crescent which is the sign of LIFE instead of the white man's cross which is the sign of slavery, suffering and death. Tell the white man that since he has not given the Negro Christian justice in his Christian religion, you are now going back to the Islamic truth of your parents . . . a religion of TRUTH that gives us dignity, unity, and makes us FEARLESS.

Elijah Muhammad maintained that the white man was the embodiment of evil, the devil incarnate. Yet the Nation did not preach aggression toward white people. Its members were not allowed to carry arms. At the same time, it warned that black people who were attacked by whites would defend themselves by "any means necessary." One member expressed the new militancy when he explained why he joined the Nation of Islam: "To get the white man's foot off my neck, his hand out of my pocket and his carcass off my back. To sleep in my own bed without fear and to look in his cold, blue eyes and call him a liar every time he parts his lips."

Many whites saw the Nation as a threat to them. During World War II, Elijah Muhammad was sent to prison for five years for encouraging his followers not to participate in a war that had nothing to do with them. In prison, he preached his message to other black prisoners.

Elijah Muhammad combined Islam, the Bible, black nationalism, racial chauvinism, military-style discipline, and bootstrap economics. He set up temples in every major city in the United States. He outlined a ten-point program for black people that included social and economic justice, equality of employment and education, freedom for black prisoners, and a separate territory for black people.

One key to Elijah Muhammad's program was self-help and self-sufficiency. The Nation of Islam stressed collective ownership of businesses. Members started many small businesses such as restaurants, dry-cleaning establishments, apartment houses, printing presses, and groceries. They were encouraged to be thrifty, honorable in their business dealings, and to gain self-respect and independence.

Many of the Nation of Islam's religious practices and beliefs were the same as those of orthodox Muslims—and remain so today. The Nation believes in Allah and his prophets. It accepts the Quran but also refers to the Bible for religious instruction even though the Nation is critical of how Christians traditionally used the Bible to oppress African-Americans. Members observe Islamic dietary laws and abstain from pork and alcohol. They also abstain from tobacco, narcotics, gambling, idleness, overeating, and oversleeping. Men and women sit in separate sections in the mosque. Women are not allowed to wear makeup or put their hair up and are required to have their head covered.

There are also differences between traditional Islam and the

*Y*oung members of the Nation of Islam usually wear formal dress for public meetings. Here a young man wears the Fruit of Islam uniform. (© Ted Gray/New York Public Library)

Nation of Islam. Members of the Nation of Islam do not pray five times a day. The Nation of Islam practices separatism, whereas Islam is a universal religion that makes no distinctions based on race. Orthodox Islam will accept neither the divinity of Fard Muhammad nor the prophecy of Elijah Muhammad. Orthodox Islam believes in the resurrection of the body on Judgment Day. But Elijah Muhammad rejected a resurrection of the body and an afterlife, preaching instead a resurrection of the mind, which frees people from ignorance, hopelessness, and despair. As Malcolm X once explained it:

> *You are the people that are dead in body. You are the people that must be resurrected in body. It doesn't mean getting up in the graveyard. It means that the power and authority and wisdom and guidance of God and His Knowledge, the knowledge of God, the understanding of God, rose up from a mentally dead people. Go home and be satisfied that you will never meet God beyond the grave. The grave settles it all. It is justice I say we want.*

The Nation of Islam had a great appeal to black men and women, many of whom saw their lives filled with despair and meaninglessness. It reached out to people in the ghettoes of America. One woman remembers how impressed she was by the teachings and behavior of a Muslim sister: "A girl in our neighborhood taught us Islam. She told us that Islam is the right religion. I believed her because of the way she dressed, the way she acted. She was different from everyone else. I wanted her to hear Islam, so I went to the Temple with my mother. My first impression was that everything she said was true."

The presence of the Nation made many people reevaluate

and dramatically change their lives. One man testifies, "In the past my life was the life of a slave. . . . Islam makes life totally worthwhile." And Sister Nellie, who was once an entertainer, states: "I thought that the life of a singer was a real life. It was a world of easy come, easy go. It was a false life, a life without security. Islam is a total way of life. It is just. It is free. You need not be a fanatic. I was always searching for something. I found it. I am a better person, a better wife."

For many men and women, belonging to the Nation of Islam changed their attitudes and behavior toward members of the opposite sex. One young woman found that there was a great difference between how women were treated in what Muslims called the "dead world" (the black community outside of Islam) and in the Nation of Islam: "I did not like the idea of adultery, drinking, smoking. You could not go places with boys without them wanting to sleep with you. In the Nation, you are not afraid of the brother. . . . When you go out with Muslim brothers, they do not make sex demands on you."

A young man who lived a promiscuous life before joining the Nation remarks: "Islam makes you appreciate women. I appreciate black women by showing them politeness and respect at its most highest degree."

Elijah Muhammad's message reached into the depths of the black community. Many who heard it were in prison or lost to drugs, alcohol, and despair. Some began to change their lives. One such man was Malcolm Little, a drug dealer and stickup man serving a ten-year sentence for grand larceny in a Massachusetts prison.

In 1947, Little received a letter from his brother telling him about the wonders of the Nation of Islam and its leader, Elijah

Muhammad. His brother explained to Malcolm the teachings of Elijah Muhammad. Malcolm liked what he heard. He agreed that the white man was the devil, something his own experience had confirmed. But as he wrote in his autobiography, it was extremely painful for him to accept God and even harder to pray. Alone in his prison cell, he forced himself to try:

> *For evil to bend its knees, admitting its guilt, to implore the forgiveness of God, is the hardest thing in the world. But then, when I was the personification of evil, I was going through it. I would force myself back down to the praying-to-Allah posture. When I was finally able to make myself stay down, I didn't know what to say to Allah.*

By the time he was ready to leave prison, Malcolm Little had been transformed into a new man by the Nation of Islam. He had taught himself how to write, talk, and think. He had given up his old life and his name and had taken on a new identity. He called himself Malcolm X.

8.

*F*rom *M*alcolm *X* to

*L*ouis *F*arrakhan

*F*or twelve years, Malcolm X had been the glory of the Nation of Islam. Brilliant, articulate, second in authority to the Honorable Elijah Muhammad, he was honored and loved by the African-American community who idolized him.

By 1961, Malcolm was the lightning rod of the Nation. The press eagerly sought him because they knew his remarks would generate controversy. He attacked whites for their racism and criticized black leaders for preaching integration during the turbulent days of civil rights. He had become an international figure, honored and respected by peoples throughout the world.

But serious problems lay underneath the surface. In his autobiography, Malcolm X claimed that members of the Nation, jealous of the attention he was receiving, spread rumors that he "was trying to take over the Nation." There was other troubling news. Malcolm said he received reports that Elijah Muhammad had committed adultery with several of his young secretaries. The two men met to discuss the matter. The meeting, according to Malcolm, was cordial, although nothing was resolved.

Malcolm X was perhaps the most famous spokesperson for the Nation of Islam before he left to form his own organization.

On November 22, 1963, President John Kennedy was assassinated. Elijah Muhammad ordered all members of the Nation not to comment on the president's death. He was afraid that someone might make a remark that would reflect badly on the Nation. Several days later, Malcolm X gave a speech about violence in America. In response to a question from the audience, Malcolm was quoted as saying that Kennedy's death was a case of "chickens coming home to roost." The press widely quoted the remark out of context and accused Malcolm of justifying Kennedy's death. The Nation of Islam was harshly criticized. Elijah Muhammad in turn criticized Malcolm for his remark. He ordered Malcolm not to speak in public for ninety days. Malcolm claimed that after he was silenced, he learned he had been marked for death.

Realizing his days with the Nation of Islam were finished, Malcolm decided to build his own organization. Feeling a strong need to broaden his knowledge of Islam, he made a pilgrimage to Mecca. Malcolm was astonished to learn that Islam as practiced by Sunni Muslims was far different from what he had learned in the Nation. The one experience that transformed him was his discovery that Islam was a "color-blind" religion. Malcolm met white Muslims whose minds were free from what he called "the white attitude." Malcolm saw Muslims of every color dressed in the simple white robes of the pilgrim—all equal, all praising God together. After his pilgrimage he publicly announced that his experiences in Mecca had changed his outlook completely:

> *During the past eleven days here in the Muslim world I have eaten from the same plate, drank from the same glass, and slept in the same bed (or on the same rug)—while praying to the same God—with fellow Muslims whose eyes were bluest of the blue, whose hair was blondest of the blonde and whose skin was whitest of the white. And in the words and in the actions and in the deeds of the white Muslims, I felt the same sincerity that I felt among the black African Muslims of Nigeria, Sudan and Ghana. . . . In the past I permitted myself to*

be used to make sweeping indictments of . . . the entire white race. . . .
Because of the spiritual enlightenment which I was blessed to receive
as a result of my recent pilgrimage to the Holy City of Mecca, I no
longer subscribe to the sweeping indictments of any one race. I am
now striving to live the life of a true Muslim.

As a result of his experience, Malcolm X changed his name to Malik El-Shabazz. In 1964 he formed the Organization of African-American Unity. It was a black nationalist organization with an Islamic orientation that was nonsectarian and nonpolitical. Its goal was to help black people, but it would not be anti-white. Many members of the Nation of Islam left to join him.

Malcolm's split from and condemnation of the Nation caused great bitterness. His house was firebombed, and he and his family were forced to flee. Louis Farrakhan, whom Malcolm had influenced to join the Nation of Islam, publicly chastised his former teacher: "Only those who wish to be led to hell, or to their doors, will follow Malcolm. . . . Such a man as Malcolm is worthy of death and would have met with it, if it had not been for Muhammad's confidence in Allah for victory of his enemies."

On February 21, 1965, Malcolm was scheduled to address a gathering at the Audubon ballroom in New York City. As he was sitting on the stage about to speak, a fight seemed to break out in the audience. "Get your hand out of my pocket!" a voice called out angrily. As Malcolm rose to calm things down, three men seated in the front row suddenly stood up. Standing in a row like a firing squad, they executed him.

The three men were arrested and convicted of the crime. Two of the men, Thomas 15X Johnson and Norman 3X Butler, were members of the Nation of Islam. They had been indicted in January for shooting another defector from the Nation. Elijah Muhammad denied that he had given the order for Malcolm's assassination. "We didn't want to kill Malcolm and we didn't try to kill him. They know I didn't harm Malcolm. They know I loved him. His foolish teaching brought him to his own end."

Some people charged that Malcolm's murder had been arranged by the FBI, who thought he had become too dangerous to white America. Minister Farrakhan suspects that the federal government played a role in the assassination. Some claim that only one of the three men convicted of the crime was actually guilty. The others responsible for the killing were never punished. In 1994, the *New York Post* suggested that Louis Farrakhan had organized Malcolm's death on orders from Elijah Muhammad. Farrakhan has vigorously denied that charge. He has publicly stated that he regrets having helped create the tense climate that may have contributed to Malcolm's death. The Nation of Islam has filed a four-billion-dollar lawsuit against the *Post* for slander.

At Malcolm's funeral, one of his friends, the actor Ossie Davis, expressed the feelings of millions of African-Americans, who respected the man for his courage even if they did not share his beliefs:

> *Malcolm was our manhood, our living black manhood. This was his meaning to our people. And in honoring him, we honor the best in ourselves. . . . And we will know him for what he is and was—a Prince—a black shining Prince—who didn't hesitate to die because he loved us so.*

Eleven years after Malcolm's assassination, Elijah Muhammad died. In 1975 he was succeeded by his son, Warith Deen Mohammed. Deen Mohammed had ideas about the future of the Nation of Islam that were far different from his father's. A student of Islam, Warith Deen Mohammed had studied Arabic, the Quran, and Islamic law for many years. He sought to bring the Nation of Islam in line with orthodox Islam. He dissolved the Fruit of Islam, temples became mosques, ministers were now imams, the Quran became the basic holy book, and all holidays were celebrated according to the Muslim calendar. He urged his followers to learn Arabic and offered courses in Arabic language and culture on a weekly television show. His followers no longer distinguished themselves from other Muslims.

Warith Deen Mohammed's goal was to bring Islam into mainstream American life. He strongly supported the United States and Saudi Arabia during the Gulf War. He also supported

Warith Deen Mohammed, the son of Elijah Muhammad, took over leadership of the Nation of Islam and became a Sunni Muslim.

Palestinian rights but criticized "terrorism or attacks on innocent people." He never publicly criticized Israel or American Jews. In 1990, he was the first Muslim imam to give the invocation before the United States Senate.

Warith Deen Mohammed's radical changes angered many of the members of the Nation of Islam. Louis Farrakhan criticized Warith Deen Mohammed for rejecting his father's teachings and making overtures to the world Muslim community. In 1978, he and his followers broke off from Warith Deen Mohammed and maintained Elijah Muhammad's original teachings and the name of the Nation of Islam. As the new leader of the Nation of Islam, Farrakhan would become one of the most controversial figures in America.

Until he joined the Nation in 1955, Farrakhan had been a musician. His name was Louis Eugene Walcott. He had made his living as a violinist, an instrument he loves and still plays today. Professionally, he performed in nightclubs under the stage name "the Charmer." He was working in Chicago when he was recruited by Malcolm X to join the Nation. Because of his outstanding personality, Farrakhan rose quickly to a position of leadership.

Dynamic, charismatic, a natural teacher and speaker, Minister Farrakhan made national headlines because of his outspoken criticism of white America and its continued oppression of black people. Because he has vigorously attacked whites as racist and Jews for using their economic and political power as landlords, merchants, and pawnbrokers to exploit blacks in the ghetto and support aggression toward Muslims, Minister Farrakhan has been called "a messenger of hate." He has been quoted as calling Judaism "a gutter religion" and praising Hitler for being "great."

Farrakhan has vigorously denied that he is anti-Semitic and racist. "You can't preach the word of God with a heart full of hatred of the white man," he once told his audience. Farrakhan has charged that the press deliberately distorts his statements. His criticism of Jews has been based on their deeds, he says, not their Jewishness. He states that he has never advocated any harm against them or ever used anti-Semitic phrases. "I have not stopped Jews from doing anything they want to do. I declared to the world that they are masquerading as the people of God. I have declared to the world that the people of God are not those who call themselves Jews, but the people of God are the black people of America, the lost, the despised, the rejected."

Farrakhan has strongly denied that he ever called Hitler a great man. He has accused his enemies of deliberately twisting what he said—that Hitler was "wickedly great," an evil man who had a great impact on the world and changed the course of history. "What kind of man would I be to praise Hitler, a man that hated black people?"

While Farrakhan has made attempts to reach out to the Jewish community, he has made it clear their relationship must be based on equality:

> *I do want to break up the old black-Jewish relationship. I don't like the old relationship where they are the landlord and we are the tenant. They have the house and we make the bed and cook the food and clean the floor. I don't want them to be the manager and we the talent. They the movie mogul and we the actor and actress, we produce something and they distribute it.*

His efforts to soften his criticisms, however, are sometimes contradicted by his followers. At Keane College in New Jersey in February of 1994, Khalid Abdul Muhammad, the national spokesperson of the Nation, lashed out at Jews, white South Africans, the pope, and homosexuals. He accused Jews of controlling the federal government and being "bloodsuckers" on his people. He also encouraged blacks in South Africa to give whites twenty-four hours to get out of the country. If they didn't leave, he said, kill them: "We kill the women, we kill the babies . . . because they will grow up to oppress our babies."

The violence of the rhetoric caused a furor, and again the Nation found itself charged with anti-Semitism and racism. Under tremendous pressure, Minister Farrakhan publicly separated himself from what Khalid Muhammad had said. "While I stand by the truths that he spoke, I must condemn in strongest terms the manner in which those terms were represented." He characterized the speech as "vile in manner, repugnant, malicious and mean spirited." At the same time, he defended the content of the speech and the speaker. He said that Jews, South Africans, and Catholics have long been oppressors of black people. He stated, "Jews cannot be held above criticism" and added that they accuse people of being anti-Semitic if they don't "bow to their will." However, he has also publicly stated that he is willing to sit down and discuss any problems with his critics as long as they don't impose preconditions for a dialogue.

Minister Conrad Muhammad, head of the New York mosque, believes that eventually the black community will forgive all those who have injured blacks:

> *At a certain point, we are going to have to forgive whites for what they did to us if we are going to move on. People get tired of hearing us cry "racism" all the time. It was effective once, but now it produces*

Minister Louis Farrakhan is a dynamic speaker who considers himself more a teacher than a spokesperson. (© Ted Gray/New York Public Library)

a backlash. We have to move forward. . . . We want justice for ourselves, and for Christians and Jews as well.

Although the media gives the impression that the Nation of Islam is obsessed with Jews and whites, most of its members' time and energy are spent supporting the organization and working in the black community. The Nation's income comes from a tithe on its members, who pay a small percentage of their income to the Nation, the sale of the organization's newspaper (the *Final Call*), and revenue from several businesses it owns (including the manufacture of beauty products and bean cakes). One main source of its income comes from government contracts for running drug and AIDS programs and providing security for federal housing units that have been plagued with crime and drugs. The Nation supplies corps of young members from the Fruit of Islam to patrol dangerous housing units in the inner cities of Baltimore, New York, Chicago, and Philadelphia. The neatly dressed (shirts, bow ties, and suit jackets), polite, serious-looking young men have, by their presence alone, deterred drug dealers from operating in some of the projects they guard. They are not always successful, but they are generally welcomed and respected by the African-American community.

The Nation is not just interested in establishing itself as a major presence in the black community. It has also become one of the most effective teaching organizations. The Nation has received national attention for being able to reach out to men and women who were leading a life of crime and abusing drugs and get them to change their ways. It works with gangs and drug dealers, trying to convince them of the error of their ways. The Nation teaches by example and through its programs, which reach out to young black and Hispanic men in the community. They do not have to be members of the Nation of Islam to participate in the special programs, although some do join. Conrad Muhammad explains:

Our focus is to reach the African-American and Hispanic youth, especially those who no one else can. We speak to high school students, sixteen, seventeen, eighteen years old. We invite them to our mosque. For many, it is a revelation. It's a kind of a meeting they have never been before. They see stern, neatly dressed, young black men speaking in a language they never heard before. We speak to them harshly about themselves and about white society. What we say may not be pleasing to the ears of whites. But it's an extreme situation that requires extreme measures. . . . It requires wisdom, compassion, and love. It's a continual struggle to live right in a wrong world.

In New York, the Nation has begun Manhood Training, a program that teaches young African-American and Hispanic men to respect themselves and others, and how to handle the daily tasks of life. In a series of classes they learn how to write checks and balance a checkbook, save money, prepare a budget, and take responsibility for a family, especially for children they father. "We explain to them," says Conrad Muhammad, "that if the parents do not love the child, it doesn't bond as it should. The baby will then grow up with no love for the father. What kind of a child will that be?"

Young people are attracted to the Nation for several reasons. One young man who has attended classes says, "I like their commitment to empowerment and to doing for self. I want to stand with them for that. I don't hate anybody." Others who are filled with anger are drawn to the militant side of the Nation. "I believe in the words of Elijah Muhammad that the white people are devils," says eighteen-year-old Nathaniel Powell. Shannon, a student at a New Jersey college who listened to both Khalid Muhammad and Louis Farrakhan speak, says she can understand why whites are upset. "The Nation of Islam is not speaking to white people. They are speaking to black people. The message is for us. We understand it and don't take it the same way as whites. They just want us to get ourselves together and be aware of what is going on around us. They don't want us to go out and kill anybody." Some see the Nation of Islam as an antidote for white racism. Tekima Berlack, a mother trying to persuade her grandson to embrace the Nation of Islam, comments, "I wasn't able to save my children from it [racism], but I'm hoping to save my grandchild. Before I close my eyes, he's going to be Farrakhan's."

The Nation of Islam also has its critics among black youth. Some object to its strong criticisms of whites and Jews and its theology. Hassan Muhammad, a university student, had read a lot about the black Muslims and was attracted by many of their doctrines. "They said things that other black leaders weren't saying about racism. They preached self-help, economic empowerment, black pride. They made you aware of what the government was doing to black men. But I didn't share their attitudes about whites." Hassan said that he lost interest in the Nation after two of its members publicly criticized some white female representatives of a children's organization he had invited to attend a meeting of an African-American group.

But even critics in the African-American community point out the hypocrisy of whites who are enraged when Minister Farrakhan makes a speech criticizing whites but are silent when officials like Senator Fritz Hollings of South Carolina make racist remarks, calling black Africans "cannibals." Farrakhan sees his mission as that of a critic in the prophetic tradition. He has called himself a "warner" who criticizes people for what they do, not for what they are. His main message is directed not to whites—despite the fact that the press focuses mainly on his controversial statements—but to the black people of America. His goal is identical to that of his teacher, the Honorable Elijah Muhammad: to save the black people from self-destruction as well as destruction by whites. He has talked to teenagers about their violence. He has condemned blacks for spending tens of billions of dollars on alcohol, drugs, and cigarettes when they could be using that money to lift themselves out of poverty. Minister Farrakhan is deeply concerned about the escalating deterioration of the black community in the United States with its single-parent

In front of City Hall in New York, members of the Nation of Islam protest an attempt by the police to force their way into the Nation of Islam mosque in response to a false alarm about a burglary in progress. There was a confrontation.

families and abandoned children. He has criticized the black man for his mistreatment of the black woman and has praised the black woman as the pillar on which the African-American community rests. Although Minister Farrakhan sees racism as the origin of his people's problems, he believes the solution lies within themselves. His message is one of self-confidence and self-help. Like Marcus Garvey, Noble Drew Ali, Fard Muhammad, Elijah Muhammad, and Malcolm X before him, Farrakhan is also saying to the African-American people, "Up you mighty race. You can conquer what you will."

Do other Muslims consider Farrakhan a Muslim? Louis Farrakhan, the leader of the Nation, at times seems to consider himself a Muslim in some ways. "I am your brother in Islam," he says. Yet there are Muslims who disagree with his theology. Hassan Muhammad, who is now a Sunni Muslim, says that he objects to the belief that Fard Muhammad is God and Elijah Muhammad his prophet. Hassan also objects to the doctrine of racial superiority that the Nation preaches, which he says is contrary to Islam's teaching about the equality of peoples. "Islam teaches that only Allah is God, and Muhammad, the last of his prophets. We believe one person may be better than another only because of his piety, not his race." Yusuf Sayyid, who is also an African-American convert to Islam, thinks that the Nation's racial doctrines give a distorted picture of what Islam is really like. Conrad Muhammad, however, feels that Middle East culture is alien to the African-American experience and that racism and corruption are still serious problems in the Arab world. He also believes that the problems of African-Americans can only be solved by African-Americans: "Only a black man can really understand our culture. You have to know our ways in order to change the condition of our people. No Arab alive can change the condition of the black man. Only those who know the black experience can do so."

Dawud Assad, head of the North American Council of Mosques, an organization whose member mosques are considered Muslim as defined by the World Council in Saudi Arabia, thinks that the Nation is moving closer to traditional Islam: "The Nation is slowly moving towards us. Farrakhan calls his churches mosques now instead of temples. He observes Ramadan at the same time we do, instead of at Christmas. So we work with him and hope that he will eventually see things from our point of view and accept Islam the way we practice it."

Whenever there is a conflict between the Nation of Islam and local authorities, many Muslims in the African-American community tend to support the Nation, even though they have religious differences.

Warith Deen Mohammed agrees. "I have to accept it as a Muslim community," he says. "We see it as one in transition, moving much slower than we did." And Imam Talib Abdur-Rashid, of the Mosque of Islamic Brotherhood in New York, notes that "in the African-American community, we do not lightly dismiss the Nation of Islam. They are an important part of our history. Many Muslims in our community would not be there if it were not for the Nation. We respect them even though we have disagreements with them. They are important in the life of our people."

9.

Sunni Islam

Many Muslims in the African-American community first learned of Islam through the Nation of Islam. But while they feel that the Nation reinforces their pride in the black community, they find orthodox Islam better meets their religious needs.

Yusuf Sayyid was not aware he was looking for a religion. Yet he was seeking something that would give meaning and purpose to his life. For a time he had been attracted to the Nation of Islam. "For a while, I felt like a God. I looked down on whites. I thought I was superior. I thought the Nation was saying the truth about society, although I never felt it was a religion." Although Yusuf had a job, on weekends he hung out with his friends, drinking and smoking pot. He was arrested for selling drugs and placed on probation. About the same time, a friend invited him to attend a meeting of an Islamic group at Rutgers University. Yusuf recalls:

I never had any religious teaching. I never had really gotten religion. When I went to that meeting, the first thing I saw was people pray-

ing. I saw people from all over the world praying together. Pakistanis, Egyptians, Indians, Arabs, whites, and African-Americans. I couldn't believe it. I stood to the side and found myself praying with them. As I prayed, I felt a change in my heart. Afterwards people came up to me and made me feel good. They treated me like a human being.

Four weeks later, Yusuf became a Muslim and gave up smoking, drinking, and drugs. At night, he "hangs out" at the mosque rather than the streets. Because he has become a practicing Muslim, he has been granted an exemption from attending a local drug program as part of the condition of his probation.

Hassan Muhammad also found his life changed after he became a Muslim. Although first attracted to the Nation because he saw Louis Farrakhan as a "black man who wasn't afraid to speak out," the more he learned about traditional Islam, the more it appealed to him. He found that Islam gave him a moral basis he was seeking in life. "Islam gave me a moral and spiritual basis on how to conduct myself. I can look at things objectively, without anger, such as the racism of some of the people I work with, who aren't even aware of their racism. Islam allows me to evaluate things according to the Quran, not on my feelings."

Hassan also discovered that racism could still be a problem among Muslims. When he met a young Egyptian woman at school and expressed interest in marrying her—and learned that she was interested in him—her parents would not consider an African-American marrying their daughter. "I felt that if her family did not want me because I was black, then I had no business being there or wanting to marry the girl."

Hassan's conversion to Islam caused conflict with his family until he married and had his first child. For Khatib Akbar Jihad, it was his children's future that led him to Islam. When they were growing up, he asked himself what was the best gift he could give them. His answer was "a moral and spiritual foundation. That was something they would have with them all their life."

Raised a Roman Catholic, Khatib Akbar began to explore various Christian denominations. None offered the spirituality he was seeking. Like many African-American men, he knew of Islam through the Nation of Islam. Through it, he discovered Sunni Islam—and found the spiritual home that he wanted for himself and his children.

> *When I was a child I remember being taught that when you died and went to heaven, you got your wings and became an angel. Well, Islam provided me with my "wings" in a spiritual sense. It gave me things way beyond what I ever expected to have. It allowed me to hear things that others do not hear, see things that others do not see, know things that others do not know. And the beauty of it is that there are still many things yet to be revealed to me.*

While many African-Americans admire Malcolm X, Elijah Muhammad, and Louis Farrakhan, they come to Islam out of their spiritual needs rather than political ones. Imam Talib Abdur-Rashid, the spiritual leader of the Mosque of Islamic Brotherhood, observes, "I would say this is the biggest change I've seen," he says. "In the sixties and seventies, many people in the African-American community were attracted to Islam because it was a means to defend the black people from being destroyed by racism. In the 1980s, they started to become Muslims because of their need for religion."

*I*mam *Talib Abdur-Rashid of the Mosque of Islamic Brotherhood shares a platform with a rabbi and a minister at a church where the theme of the talk was cooperation among the three faiths.*

Most African-Americans are converts to Islam. After conversion, many take an Arabic name, often choosing the names of great Muslims of the past to inspire them in daily life. Muhammad is one of the most common because it is the name of the Prophet himself. The names of some of the Prophet's relatives are also popular, such as his nephew, Ali, his grandsons, Hasan and Hussein, two of his wives, Khadija and Zainab, and his daughter, Fatimah. Ali was also a great Muslim general—which was the reason the heavyweight champion Muhammad Ali took the name when he became a member of the Nation of Islam.

Some names reflect one of the ninety-nine attributes that

Muslims believe are qualities of Allah. Karim means "generous"; Jamil means "beautiful"; Rahman, "gracious" or "beneficent." Since no one but Allah has these attributes in their fullness, the name is modified by using the word *abdul,* meaning "the servant of." Thus the meaning of the name of the famous basketball player Kareem (generous) Abdul (servant of) Jabbar (mighty) is "generous servant of the mighty."

Imam Abdur-Rashid's community represents an average African-American Muslim community in many ways. He is the imam of the Mosque of Islamic Brotherhood, located in Harlem, New York. The mosque was founded by Shaykhul-Allama Tawfiq, a friend and associate of Malcolm X. Shaykhul-Allama Tawfiq was one of the first American Muslims to be invited to study Islam at Al-Azhar in Cairo, Egypt, the major center for Islamic studies in the Muslim world.

The building in which the Mosque for Islamic Brotherhood holds its religious services is a brownstone converted into a mosque. The building is one of several owned by the congregation. It is in the process of being renovated into a religious center, an Islamic school, and apartments for mostly Muslim families. There are also plans to convert one of the other buildings into an overnight shelter for the homeless. Since most Muslim congregations do not have the financial resources to build a traditional mosque, it is not unusual for Muslims to convert buildings, lofts, apartments, and storefronts into places of worship.

The Mosque of Islamic Brotherhood is sometimes perceived as a threat to the drug dealers in the neighborhood because of Islam's strong prohibition against drugs and alcohol. For Hamza Tawfiq, a teenager, being a Muslim did create problems with some of his peers in the community: "They said that we [Muslims] thought we were better than them. They challenged us. Some threw snowballs at us that had rocks in them. We had to stand up for what we believed." Yet others are glad there is a mosque in the area because it does command respect for the righteous way in which its members live.

The Mosque of Islamic Brotherhood has a membership of seventy-five families. The first responsibility of the imam is to meet the spiritual needs of his community (_ummah_). On Friday, he leads the congregation in prayer. On Sundays, he teaches Arabic so that the members can eventually read the Quran in Ara-

_P_art of the imam's responsibility to his congregation is to teach Arabic in order that men and women in his congregation can read the Quran in its original language.

bic. Equally important is the *dawa*, which literally means "invitation" and is often loosely translated as "propagation of the faith." Every Muslim is obligated to make Islam known to others so that they may have the opportunity to accept it. Dawa does not mean forcing anyone to convert.

Imam Talib Abdur-Rashid is also the imam at Sing Sing Prison, located in Ossining, New York. Over 2,000 men are incarcerated here, 400 of whom have identified themselves as Muslims. The active Muslim community numbers about 200.

Why does Islam appeal to men in prison? "Because it provides a refuge from the storm of prison life," one inmate replies. A prison for men is an antihuman environment. It is a closed, all-male society, in which many are violent men who have been involved in a life of crime and drugs.

Rafiq has been incarcerated for twenty-five years for a murder he insists he didn't commit. He turned to Islam to protect his integrity. Like many men in prison, Rafiq was introduced to Islam through the Nation of Islam. Although he is now a member of the Sunni Muslim community of Warith Deen Mohammed, he is forever grateful to the Nation of Islam for what it did for him.

I was deeply impressed with the brothers in the Nation. They showed us discipline. They showed us self-respect. I was blessed to have such teachers. They had lots of substance. They accepted themselves. They didn't have moral corruption. They were clean. They bathed and exercised. They studied. They didn't accept excuses. They were soldiers. Seeing them made you want to be like them.

Rafiq believes the Nation of Islam plays a positive role in prisoners' lives. It gives them the strength to deal with the many

*A*bout 200 *men incarcerated at Sing Sing prison are Sunni Muslims. They have converted empty rooms into a mosque and a center for study.*

problems that people experience once they are imprisoned—especially men serving life sentences.

> *Men suffer a lot in prison, but you never hear about it. They suffer when their mothers die, when a favorite sister dies, when a wife divorces them. They suffer when their children go to jail. And they have to deal with all that pain themsleves. Islam has a lot of solutions to the problems that men complain about. That's why it's so attractive to many men in prison.*

One of the goals that Muslims like Rafiq set for themselves is to help younger men coming into prison to get off the prison

track. The best way that Rafiq feels he can reach them is by
setting an example:

> *You can't just preach to these kids. You have to be sincere. You can't*
> *tell them not to do something that you do yourself. You cannot make*
> *progress if you're ignorant. You can't have the same weakness. You*
> *have to be strong to be in prison. Mentally strong. Physically*
> *strong. People respect strength. Muslims in prison have both qualities*
> *that every prisoner respects, intelligence and courage.*

Imam Abdur-Rashid also works with men after they have
been released from prison. Some abandon Islam after they get

*Imam Talib Abdur-Rashid meets with Rafiq, a lifer at Sing Sing. The imam is the Muslim
chaplain for the prison.*

out and return to their old way of life, whereas others try to hold on and make something of their lives. He has seen violent men he has worked with in prison walk away from a confrontational situation even though they felt the impulse to kill or injure an opponent.

> *I was at a street fair, and I saw this man who had been released from prison having a heated argument with someone. He was a pretty violent man, and he had converted to Islam while in prison. I watched him as he walked away from the other man and paced up and down the street for ten minutes before he cooled down. In the past, I know he would have gone and gotten his gun and shot the man. I walked over to him and congratulated him on getting his temper under control.*

While the Mosque of Islamic Brotherhood is not nationalistic, it is very deeply involved in the black community. Whenever there is an injustice or abuse to black people, Imam Talib Abdur-Rashid is quick to respond. When the unarmed son of an Islamic leader in Brooklyn was shot and killed by a police officer, the imam helped organize a protest demanding an independent investigation of the circumstances. When the police entered a mosque of the Nation of Islam in violation of their rule that no weapons were allowed inside the mosque, and a scuffle broke out in which police officers were injured, Imam Abdur-Rashid was one of a group of imams to stage a demonstration against the police at City Hall. He and other Muslims and non-Muslims were angry that the police entered a Muslim sanctuary without following the proper guidelines. "Had it been a church or synagogue, they never would have dared to do it. But they think they can get away with it when it's a mosque. That's unacceptable as far as we are concerned."

The imam speaks to many Jewish and Christian groups, explaining Islam and trying to build interfaith unity. (He faced a severe setback after a Jewish gunman entered a mosque in Hebron in the West Bank occupied by Israel and machine-gunned the congregation at prayer during Ramadan, killing forty people. Several days later, in retaliation, a Lebanese-born gunman allegedly fired at a school bus carrying orthodox Jewish students in New York, killing one and wounding several others. Reacting quickly to this crisis, the imam joined forces with a rabbi and a minister to call for calm and peace in New York.) He tries to show how Islam is becoming an influential force in American political life, partly as a result of the activism of the African-American Muslim community. He also explains why Islam has such a large appeal in the African-American community.

Once considered a religion for the poor, today Islam attracts men and women from all stations in life. There are African-American Muslim police officers, computer programmers, post office employees, business executives, and college professors. In Kountze, Texas, a town that is 70 percent white and in which there are only two Muslim families, the mayor is an African-American Muslim. The first Muslim chaplain has recently been appointed in the United States Army.

There is no question that Sunni Islam is having an impact on the African-American community and will continue to do so. The next stage in its development perhaps will be to draw closer to the immigrant Muslim community. As Imam Abdur-Rashid points out:

The strength of Islam lies in its unity and that it cuts across all ethnic divisions. Too many Muslims still think nationally instead of universally. The more united we are, the stronger we will be . . . and the more influence we will have on American life. My feeling is that in the next few decades, a larger number of Americans will find their way to Islam because I believe it has the answers to the questions most people here are asking.

Conclusion

*I*n the past, Muslim immigrants identified very strongly with their own ethnic communities. They isolated themselves from Muslim African-Americans. Today this division is breaking down. On any given Sunday, in most Islamic centers throughout the United States, Muslims of every ethnic background pray and socialize together. Many congregations are inviting African-Americans to join. Ibrahim Sidicki, a college student whose family is from India, notes that "as young people start to take control of their mosque, they will make it a priority to merge closer with the African-American community." On college campuses, this has already happened. Yusuf Sayyid, an African-American Muslim, comments, "One of the things that I love about Islam is that it is so diverse." Warith Deen Mohammed, leader of one of the largest African-American Muslim communities, was recently the keynote speaker at a convention of the Islamic Society of North America (ISNA). ISNA is the largest Muslim umbrella organization in the United States and Canada. Most of its members are Muslims whose roots are in the Middle

East and Asia. Both ISNA and Warith Deen Mohammed have announced plans for eventually holding a joint convention.

For many Muslims, whether they are American-born or born overseas, there is still a strong identification with fellow Muslims around the world. Muslims have their roots in countries experiencing great upheavals and suffering. In Kashmir, Muslims are being killed by Hindus; in Bosnia, they are being slaughtered by Christian Serbs. There is civil war in Afghanistan. For almost five decades, war has raged between Palestinians and Israelis, although an end may now be in sight. In other countries, there are dictatorships that oppress people or conflicts between religious militants and government authorities as are taking place in Egypt and Algeria.

Contributing to the turbulence in the Muslim world has been the rise of radical groups with names such as Those Saved from Hell, The Army of Muhammad, Islamic Bugle, and The Holy War Party. Such groups see violence as a religious duty. They want to replace governments that they find oppressive, corrupt, and illegitimate with social justice based on the Quran. Many of the militants are anti-West. They see Europe and America as colonial powers whose corrupt value system is hostile to Islam. Americans are sometimes startled to see on their television screens images of Iranian revolutionaries chanting "Death to America!" To most Americans, it seems fanatical, especially when Americans are killed.

Ayesha Kezmi, a high school student, feels that American Muslims have an obligation to take action on behalf of Muslims who are suffering in other countries. "When you see Muslims killed in other parts of the world, it hurts. You want to do something to help." Ayesha has been trying to enter Bosnia to help

Muslims who have suffered from Serbian brutality. "I want peace with justice. I want to let people know what Muslims are going through in Bosnia." Like other Muslims, Ayesha peacefully demonstrates on behalf of Bosnians. She is critical to those Muslims who refuse to get involved because they do not want to call attention to themselves.

Jim Zogby, who heads a political organization that lobbies for Arab and Muslim causes, sees American Muslims as being in a good position to help Muslims in other countries: "American Muslims have the opportunity to be the most influential in the world. They have the opportunity to offer people abroad what

Young Muslims, many of whom come from immigrant families, identify themselves as American Muslims. "The United States," according to one student, "is the best place to practice Islam."

they cannot have because of political circumstances, oppression, poverty, or education."

On a national level, the United States has at times become deeply involved in the Islamic world. During the 1980s, American troops were sent to Lebanon to keep the peace in a bitter civil war. Two hundred and fifty marines were killed when a man drove a truck filled with explosives into an American compound. America supported Muslim militants in Afghanistan in their war against the Soviet army that had occupied their country. American naval ships patrolling the Persian Gulf during a conflict with Iran shot down, by mistake, an Iranian commercial airliner, killing over 300 people. An air strike was launched against Libya in an attempt to assassinate its president, Muammer Khadafi. In 1991, the United States openly attacked Iraq, forcing it to withdraw from Kuwait.

In retaliation, militants occasionally struck at American targets abroad. The worst incident was the bombing of an American plane in midflight in 1987 in which 270 were killed. The year 1993 brought terrorism home to America with the World Trade Center bombing. Four Muslims were convicted of the crime. This was followed by an FBI raid on a group of Muslims who were charged with conspiring to bomb major tourist centers such as the Statue of Liberty in New York.

Whenever such incidents happen, American Muslims immediately suffer the consequences. They are labeled as "terrorists," "fundamentalists," and "radicals." During the Gulf War, hate messages were left on the answering machine at the Islamic Center in San Diego, California. "Why don't you terrorists go back to your own country?" "Get out of America!" "You're not Americans!" "You don't belong here." In Los Angeles, California, vandals spray-painted the house of an Iranian family with the slogan. "Go back home!" The furniture inside the house was slashed with a knife, urine was left in the sink, and the garage was destroyed. Women wearing the hejab have been insulted on the street. During the Gulf War in 1991, hate crimes, arsons, bombings, and assaults against Arab-Americans rose from thirty-nine the previous year to 119.

The threats intimidate some. "I am almost afraid to tell people that I am a Muslim," Samir El Sayed says. Few Muslims openly support such terrorist tactics, and the majority condemn them. However, others are not too concerned. One man described the World Trade Center bombing as no more than "a passing cloud on a sunny day."

But even though there is hostility, the numbers of Muslims in America continue to increase. The majority are the new generations of Muslim children being born. Many are immigrants. The number of Muslims entering the country each year is not officially known because immigration officials do not ask a person's religion. In 1991, 100,000 legal immigrants came from countries whose Muslim populations are 90 percent or more. At the same time, more Americans are converting to Islam.

Today, Muslims in the United States are increasingly emphasizing their American identity rather than their ethnic backgrounds. They are Democrats and Republicans, liberals and conservatives. They wish to prosper, raise families, practice their religion without interference, and contribute to the society in which they live. "The best place to be a Muslim," says Sana al-Janabi, "is in America." She is Egyptian-American, and, although born and raised in America, she has visited her parents' homeland many times. She believes that she is a better Muslim here in an open, democratic society than she would be in a restricted one. Muhammad al-Marayati, an Iraqi-American, expresses the feelings of many when he says:

> We are part of this country. We feel proud of our American Islamic identity. We want to be part of the mosaic. We don't consider ourselves as belonging to the Middle East or to South Asia. Our roots may be there, but our present and future are here. We are looking forward to the day when Americans will define the United States as a Protestant, Catholic, Jewish, and Muslim country.

Bibliography

The quotations that appear in this book are taken from the author's interviews with a cross section of Muslims throughout the United States and from the sources listed below, which are recommended for further reading.

The best general history of the life of Muhammad, the Arab peoples, and the rise of Islamic civilization is:

Hourani, Albert. *A History of the Arab Peoples*. Cambridge, Mass.: The Belknap Press of Harvard University, 1991.

For the Arab point of view of the Crusades, see:

Gabreillia, Francesco. *Arab Historians of the Crusades*. Berkeley and Los Angeles: University of California Press, 1969.
Usamah Ibn-Munqidh. *An Arab-Syrian Gentleman and Warrior in the Period of the Crusades*. Translated from the original manuscript by Phillip Hitti. New York: Columbia University Press, 1929.

Bibliography

For the Christian perspective on the Crusades, refer to:

Armstrong, Karen. *The Crusades and Their Impact on Today's World.* New York: Anchor, Doubleday, 1988.

For the religion of Islam, a good introduction is:

Matar, N. I. *Islam for Beginners.* New York: Writers and Readers Publishing, 1992.

For Islam in America today, see:

Haddad, Yvonne Yazbeck. *The Muslims of America.* New York: Oxford University Press, 1991.
Mallison, Elias. *Neighbors: Muslims in North America.* New York: Friendship Press, 1989.

For the most complete history of Islam in the African-American community up to the Civil War, see:

Allen, Austin. *African Muslims in Antebellum America: A Sourcebook.* New York and London: Garland Publishing, 1984.

For the period after the Civil War:

Essien-Udon, I. E. *Black Nationalism: A Search for Identity in America.* Chicago: University of Chicago Press, 1962.

For the Nation of Islam, refer to:

Farrakhan, Louis. *A Torchlight for America.* Chicago: FCN Publishing, 1993.

Bibliography

Lincoln, Eric C. *The Black Muslims in America*. Boston: Beacon Press, 1973.

Malcolm X (Malik El-Shabbaz), and Haley, Alex. *The Autobiography of Malcolm X*. New York: Grove Press, 1964.

Muhammad, Elijah. *Message to the Black Man*. Chicago: Temple Number 6, 1965.

Index

Index

Index